The Human Side of Change

Timothy J. Galpin

The Human Side of Change

A Practical Guide to Organization Redesign

JOSSEY-BASS
A Wiley Company
San Francisco

Jossey-Bass books and products are available through most bookstores. To contact Jossey-Bass directly, call (888) 378-2537, fax to (800) 605-2665, or visit our website at www.josseybass.com.

Substantial discounts on bulk quantities of Jossey-Bass books are available to corporations, professional associations, and other organizations. For details and discount information, contact the special sales department at Jossey-Bass.

Manufactured in the United States of America on Lyons Falls
TCF Turin Book. This paper is acid-free and 100 percent totally chlorine-free.

Library of Congress Cataloging-in-Publication Data

Galpin, Timothy J.
  The human side of change : a practical guide to organization redesign / Timothy J. Galpin. — 1st ed.
    p.   cm. — (The Jossey-Bass business & management series)
  Includes bibliographical references and index.
  ISBN 0-7879-0216-0 (acid-free paper)
  1. Organizational change—Psychological aspects.   I. Title.
II. Series.
  HD58.8.G35   1996
  658.4'06—dc20   95-47039

HB Printing   10 9 8 7 6 5   FIRST EDITION

Contents

Preface   xiii

The Author   xix

Introduction: The Change Management Process   1
- *A Model of the Change Management Process* • *Summary*

**Part One: At the Strategic Level:
Organizationwide Change Management Imperatives**

1. Teams: Building the Infrastructure
   for Effective Change   17
   - *Establishing a Coordinated Team Infrastructure* • *The
   Steering Committee* • *The Integration Team* • *Improvement
   Teams* • *Teams Create Better Results than Individuals*
   • *Improvement Team Membership* • *Improvement Team
   Operations* • *The Improvement Team Process* • *Team
   Principles* • *Effective Team Facilitation* • *Team Record
   Keeping* • *Summary*

2. Communications: Beating the Grapevine
   with an Open Two-Way Strategy   33
   - *A Framework for Organizational Communication*
   • *Communication Fundamentals* • *Avoiding Common
   Pitfalls* • *Communication Helps Lower Resistance*
   • *Phases of the Communication Process* • *Specifics*
   • *Summary*

3. Culture: Managing All the Components   53
    • *Operationalizing Organizational Culture* • *Managing
    Organizational Culture During Change* • *Applying a Cultural
    Screen* • *Identifying Implementation Actions* • *Developing
    Action Plans* • *Implementing the Actions* • *Measuring the
    Impact* • *Continuing to Manage Cultural Components to
    Reinforce Change* • *Summary*

4. Leadership: Developing the
    Key Attributes for Leading Change   67
    • *Relationship Power Versus Position Power* • *Key
    Attributes for Leading Change* • *Behavioral Change for
    Leaders* • *Summary*

**Part Two: At the Grassroots Level:
Implementing and Sustaining Change**

5. Set Goals   81
    • *Understanding and Communicating the Changes That
    Will Take Place* • *Setting Goals* • *Guidelines for Effective
    Goal Setting* • *Summary*

6. Measure Performance   93
    • *Guidelines for Effective Measurement* • *What Does
    Measurement Look Like?* • *Summary*

7. Provide Feedback and Coaching   101
    • *What Do Feedback and Coaching Look Like?* • *Guidelines
    for Effective Coaching* • *A Coaching Tip* • *Summary*

8. Be Generous with Rewards and Recognition   109
    • *The Difference Between Rewards and Recognition*
    • *Guidelines for Effective Rewards and Recognition* • *What
    Do Rewards and Recognition Look Like?* • *Summary*

Conclusion: The Tough Questions
of Change Management 117

The Change Manager's Toolkit

Appendix A: Strategic Toolkit 123

Appendix B: Implementation Toolkit 129

Appendix C: Glossary of Terms 135

Appendix D: Recommended Readings 137

Index 143

Preface

The topic of organizational change is not new. Mergers throughout the 1980s, downsizing and restructuring during the first few years of the 1990s, and the business process reengineering craze of today—encompassing huge leaps in information technology—have all thrust change into the forefront of the organizational consciousness. However, the way in which organizations go about creating change is new. During their mergers, downsizings, and restructurings, most organizations have focused on the technical, financial, and operational aspects of change with little regard for the human side of the process. At best blundering through and at worst ignoring this "soft side" of change has led many organizational change efforts down a rocky road and into severe pitfalls. These pitfalls have manifested themselves in the form of labor relations problems, loss of key people and talent, and little or no benefits from the change efforts.

With all that has been written about organizational change recently, it seems surprising that organizations continue to find themselves encountering severe problems. In just one database search I identified 1,789 articles or books that fell under the heading of "organizational change." Furthermore, the search was limited to material published since January 1994. But a review of this material shows that much of it focuses on analytical techniques, such as cost-benefit analysis, cost per unit analysis, activity-based costing, cycle time analysis, error rates tracking, scale curves, and so on.

This type of material is often more practical and tangible in nature than the material dealing with the human side of change.

Unfortunately, a review of the writing about the soft aspects of change shows that these materials are often conceptual, theoretical, or anecdotal in nature with only a few ineffectual presentations of a how-to type.

This Book's Purpose and Audience

The purpose of *The Human Side of Change* is to provide readers with a pragmatic approach to addressing the soft aspects of change. The book is designed to illustrate clearly to senior executives, midlevel managers, and frontline supervisors ways in which they can navigate through the pitfalls surrounding the human elements of change. The contents are based on my numerous experiences with change efforts in both commercial and governmental organizations. These experiences continually support the conviction that combining the soft side with the technical side of change creates an effective and lasting transformation.

Throughout *The Human Side of Change*, I have tried to bridge the gap between theory and practice. The language of the text is meant to be straightforward and unacademic, with little "consultantese."

The book is intended to be used as a how-to manual for organizations either currently undertaking or preparing to embark on a change effort. A framework as well as numerous tools, techniques, examples, and two "users' guides"—or toolkits—are included to assist management at every step through the thorny issues that occur when addressing the human side of change.

Overview of the Book

The book begins with an introductory chapter and then is separated into two parts. The introduction presents a model of the change management process. The components of the change management model help to introduce the key soft side characteristics of each stage of the change process.

Part One addresses the soft aspects of change that are broad, organizationwide, and strategic in nature. Part One is designed to guide senior executives and top managers as they manage change across their organizations. Chapter One addresses the fundamentals of leveraging the power of a team approach to change, including the steps teams must work through while creating recommendations for change. Chapter Two outlines a practical approach to developing and implementing an organizationwide communication strategy during change. The chapter presents a context from which to approach communication during change, some do's and don'ts, and a step-by-step approach to developing a solid communication strategy. Chapter Three presents a pragmatic approach to linking organizational culture to the change effort to help effectively implement and sustain it. Chapter Four deals with the key leadership attributes that help effect successful change and offers a behavioral approach to shape the leadership skills of management.

Part Two describes the management of the soft side of change that takes place at the lower levels of organizations. Part Two is written to guide middle managers and supervisors as they implement and sustain change under their spans of control. Chapters Five, Six, Seven, and Eight describe, one by one, the four stages of a change implementation model, along with the actions to take during each stage. These four chapters focus on the grass roots of change in an organization. Finally, the conclusion summarizes the key messages of each chapter in Parts One and Two.

In order to assist readers in applying the tools and techniques presented in each chapter, two users' guides are provided as appendixes. Appendix A, the Strategic Toolkit, is designed for executives and senior managers to use to work through the strategic aspects of a change initiative: establishing a need to change, developing a vision of change, establishing a change infrastructure, implementing a communication strategy, linking organizational culture to recommended changes, and leading a change process.

Appendix B addresses the grassroots aspects of implementing change. This Implementation Toolkit focuses on goal setting, measuring, reinforcing, and refining changes. It was designed to help middle managers and supervisors manage the soft side of change in their areas to support the organizationwide change effort and effectively play their parts in achieving the goals of a change initiative.

As a further aid to readers, the numbers of the questions in the two appendixes that correspond to the techniques, actions, and tools presented in each chapter are referenced throughout the text. Likewise, the numbers of the chapters corresponding to each question are noted in the appendixes next to each question.

A glossary is also included. It defines key terms used within the text.

For additional reference, a recommended reading list is also provided. The books and articles listed are categorized by topic to help readers find more information about specific areas of the soft side of change, including general material on organizational change and information on teams, communications, change leadership, culture change, goals, measurement, feedback and coaching, and rewards and recognition.

Acknowledgments

No work, however large or small, ever represents the knowledge of one person alone. This book is no exception. The text reflects insights, concepts, and experiences collected from numerous people who come from both an American and an international business perspective. Colleagues, clients, friends, and family all provided their insights and comments to add to my understanding and approach to the topic of change. I do not include the specific names of these "contributors" as there are many and I know I would leave key people off the list. I trust that they will accept a simple thank you as an expression of my gratitude and appreciation.

Dallas, Texas   Timothy J. Galpin
January 1996

To my mother, Elizabeth Mary Costa Galpin

The Author

Timothy J. Galpin is a principal with the consulting division of Pritchett & Associates, Inc., in Dallas, Texas. He received his Ph.D. degree in organization development from the University of California, Los Angeles, and has extensive experience in industry and consulting in both North America and Europe.

Galpin has led projects incorporating the design, implementation, and evaluation of business process redesign, productivity improvement, customer service enhancement, and strategic planning that have resulted in improved performance for international firms and public sector organizations. He has published several articles dealing with performance improvement, change management, and organizational productivity.

The Human
Side of
Change

The Change Management Process

In order for an organizational change effort to be successful, two levels of change must be addressed: the strategic level and the grassroots level. As defined in this text, the term *strategic change* is not meant to convey large-scale, sweeping change, nor is *grassroots change* intended to mean small, incremental improvement. Rather, the terms refer to the two levels of change that occur during a change effort within an organization.

Strategic change denotes the up-front, initial effort involving executives, senior managers, a small cadre of employees, and often consultants, who provide an outside view. Strategic change is broad and organizationwide. There are two primary goals during the strategic change phase: a technical or analytical goal and what I call a "soft side" goal. The primary technical goal is the generation of recommendations for change. The primary soft side goal is the establishment of the momentum for change.

During the strategic change phase, analytical tools and techniques are applied. Analytics include cost-benefit analyses, cost per unit analyses, activity-based costing, cycle time analyses, error rate analyses, scale curves, flow charts, surveys, interviews, benchmarks, and so on. But it is not the purpose of this text to address these techniques. Instead, this book intends to present the reader with the soft side techniques that can be applied to begin managing the human aspects of strategic change and create momentum. The soft side tools and techniques presented in this chapter and the chapters that make up Part One of the book (Chapters One through Four) are for use by the senior executives and top managers of organizations.

They will be helpful to the leaders of both public and private organizations. These soft side tools and techniques include establishing a need to change and develop a vision of where the change should go (Introduction), establishing a change infrastructure (Chapter One), developing and implementing a communication strategy (Chapter Two), linking organizational culture to recommended changes (Chapter Three), and developing the leadership characteristics critical to creating a successful change process (Chapter Four).

Grassroots change is the effort that drives change deep into an organization. It stresses implementation at the local level. The primary goal of the grassroots change phase is to implement and sustain desired changes. Part Two (Chapters Five through Eight) examines the tools and techniques that middle managers and frontline supervisors can use to effect change within their spans of control. These include setting goals (Chapter Five), performing measurements (Chapter Six), providing coaching and feedback (Chapter Seven), and offering rewards and recognition (Chapter Eight).

Effectively managing both the strategic and grassroots levels of change can mean the difference between success and failure. It can produce millions of dollars in savings and increase revenues. The requirements, level of involvement, and goals of each level of change differ fundamentally from each other. The key differences are presented in Table I.1.

As shown in the table, the differences between strategic and grassroots change lie in the scope of the effort, the people most deeply involved, and the outcome goals for each level of change. Leadership for strategic change comes from senior levels of the organization. Small teams of selected individuals are often involved. Using broad diagnostics and analytics together with external benchmarking and best-practice comparisons, they begin to chart a course, to make recommendations, and to establish the momentum for change. Grassroots change involves many more people. The leadership comes from senior executives, middle management, and frontline supervisors. During grassroots change, individual and team goals are set; measurements are

**Table I.1. The Differences
Between Strategic and Grassroots Change.**

	Strategic Change	Grassroots Change
Leadership	Top management	Local management
Infrastructure	A select few	Management, employees, "the masses"
Diagnostics	The entire organization	Specific sites
Comparison points	Comparison of external benchmarking and best practices to internal	Implementation of best practices
Tools (process mapping, surveys, activity-based costing, and so on)	Introduction and application of data collection tools and techniques to a select few	Application of implementation tools to "the masses"
Training	Assessment of needs, some design and delivery	Assessment of needs, extensive design and delivery
Outcome goals	Recommendations for change and momentum building	Implementation of changes

developed; people are trained and coached in new techniques, procedures, and technologies; reinforcement is established; and changes are implemented.

A Model of the Change Management Process

To the dismay of many executives, change does not occur in one great leap. Whether a change effort is focused on operational procedures, manufacturing processes, organizational restructuring, total quality management, financial processes, or administrative cost reduction, successful change efforts entail several key stages along the way. Figure I.1 depicts a change process model that defines nine stages for creating and implementing organizational change.

Figure I.1. The Change Management Process Model.

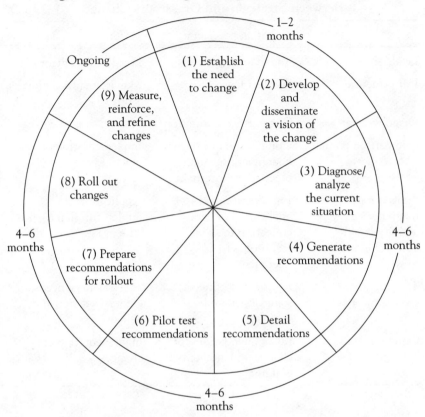

Note: The times shown for each stage and the cumulative time of thirteen to twenty months for all stages will vary depending on the scope and complexity of the change effort.

The stages identified in the figure are generalizable to many different types of change efforts and the time frames associated with each stage are typical for major change efforts (that is, those involving multiple functions or areas of the organization). As the figure indicates, the nine stages can take upwards of twenty months to conduct. The time frame will vary depending on the scope and complexity of the effort.

In the first stage of the change process model the need to change is established. (Appendix A, Strategic Toolkit, questions 1 to 3.) Identifying and articulating the need to change helps people understand why the changes are needed. The rationale for change that is expressed may include but need not be limited to the desire for excellence; a reaction to competitive pressures, benchmarks from other companies, or customer requests; a need for decreased cycle time; and a need for cost reduction. In addition, the consequences of not changing should be made clear. While defining the need to change, supporting facts should be gathered that underline the reasons to change. For example, a large oil and chemical company used industry benchmarks to compare the cost of its support functions (such as systems, purchasing, finance, human resources, real estate, planning, legal, and so on) with the amount that other companies were spending on the same support functions. The company learned that its support functions were 20 percent to 40 percent more costly than those of other companies of similar size and complexity. The management of the company used these comparisons as part of its rationale for and communication of the initiation of an organizationwide business process reengineering (BPR) effort aimed at reducing the cost of the support functions. This example illustrates how analytical change tools (in this case benchmarking) can be combined with soft side techniques (communicating a need to change) at the outset of strategic change.

The second stage of the change process shown in the model—developing and disseminating a vision of the change—is essential to establish a picture of what the organization will look like when the change is successful. (Appendix A, Strategic Toolkit, questions 4 through 7.) A clear vision for change helps people see where the organization seeks to go. In addition, a vision helps communicate the value of change to the organization. The vision should be expressed in a way that allows all people in the organization to understand it, relate to it, and see their roles in achieving it. Moreover, the vision for change should stretch the organization and the people within it while at the same time be perceived as attainable. Which people are involved in developing the vision depends on the scope of the change. A vision for organizationwide efforts should be developed by senior leaders; more narrowly focused visions for change can be developed at division or operating unit levels. As shown in Figure I.2, the vision of change must expand as the scope and magnitude of change increases.

Once a vision is developed, it must be disseminated throughout the organization so that management and employees alike can understand and buy into it. This process is still part of stage two of the model. A number of methods can help establish buy in, ranging from announcements to an interactive and personal approach. There are advantages and disadvantages to each approach. The announcement method is useful in larger organizations where executive contact with the masses may not be feasible or in an organization where people are already on board with the change process. In contrast, the interactive approach is useful when there is little buy in to the change process or in smaller organizations where greater interaction with senior management is logistically possible. A combination of the two approaches—or "cascading" the vision of change—often works well.

An example of cascading a change vision is the following. The new chairman of a large retail organization wanted to launch a customer service improvement process for over ten thousand sales staff located in approximately one thousand stores scattered across the

Figure I.2. The Vision of Change.

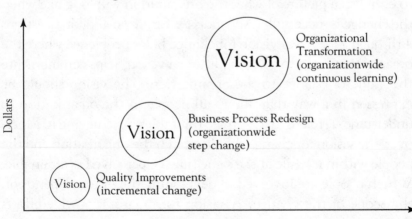

United States. The size and geographic diversity of this company made it physically impossible for the chairman to get to all locations in a reasonable period of time. Instead, the company used a cascade approach to disseminate the vision and kick off the process over a four-week time frame. First, the chairman held an interactive meeting—a dialogue—with the top executives in the company to explain his vision of the customer service changes, the rationale behind it, and the approach that would be taken to achieve it. The meeting allowed ample time for discussion. Coming out of the meeting, the senior management team was required to hold similar meetings with the middle management teams reporting directly to each of them. Each senior manager was asked to use the same type of interactive approach to disseminate the customer service vision and approach. To help prepare for their meetings and to ensure consistency as the vision "cascaded" down, the executives were provided with a meeting outline. In addition, they were required to hold their meetings within a week of the meeting with the chairman. Within a week of this second tier of meetings, all midlevel managers were required to hold a meeting with their direct reports; they too were provided with a meeting outline. Finally, the managers and supervisors participating in these meetings were required to hold interactive meetings with their employees. Each cascading level of meetings had interaction built in, allowing ample time for questions between participants and those delivering the message.

Whichever communication method is chosen—announcements or interactive meetings—the approach should be one that is appropriate for the size of the organization and level of buy in that currently exists to the vision being communicated.

In the third stage, the procedures that currently exist in the organization are diagnosed or analyzed and the findings compared with the desired vision of change. This stage is characterized by the broad application of various diagnostics and analytics. As mentioned earlier, numerous techniques and tools are available to help in the analyses of the current organizational situation (for example, cost-benefit analyses, cycle time analyses). Again, it is not the purpose of this text to address these analytical techniques. Organizations can provide their employees with the knowledge and skills of these tools and techniques through several sources, including textbooks, articles, business school courses and programs, internal training classes, and training by outside consultants.

The key during the analysis stage of the change process is to build a comprehensive picture of the current process or area of the organization being examined. A comprehensive analysis provides data that can be used during strategic change in three important ways. First, analysis highlights processes that can be improved by streamlining, elimination, consolidation, and automation. This leads to the next two stages of the model—generating ideas and making recommendations. Second, the data can be used to support the need to change, as defined during the discussion of stage one. Third, the information can be used as a baseline, or comparison point, when assessing the impact of changes that are eventually implemented. However, it is important not to get bogged down in the analysis and the data. Although these uses of the data are important during a change process, a focus on gathering too much data will impede progress and diminish the intended outcomes of a change initiative.

The analysis stage is also a good time to begin the elements of grassroots change by involving employees in the effort. They can be asked to assist with data collection, to participate in surveys, interviews, or focus groups, or to participate in meetings. In large organizations or large segments of a business, every employee may not be able to participate personally. However, representatives can be involved who then become "ambassadors" of the change effort.

During stage four of the change process recommendations are generated. Ideas are raised to improve, eliminate, combine, and develop new processes. Idea generation should be an open market on creativity. Often, best-practice comparisons and benchmarking are sources for new ways of operating. Employees who do the work being examined are another excellent source of improvement ideas. They can add to the creative process through participation in written surveys, interviews, or focus groups. Involving employees during the idea generation stage will begin to reinforce the process of grassroots change.

Once recommendations are generated, details need to be added to them—stage five in the change process. Details include costs, hardware and software availability, equipment needs, maintenance considerations, training needs, and the like. In addition, this is the stage when ideas should be evaluated based on their merits, that is, cost effectiveness, time of implementation, available technology, and so on.

Pilot testing occurs at stage six. The pilot testing stage is when grassroots change becomes more important as improvements are tried out within the organization. Although some changes don't lend themselves to testing—for example, the reorganization of an entire division or the redesign of an entire process that cuts across several areas of the organization—many changes do. Pilot testing does not have to encompass an entire process. Key segments of improvements may be tested in a limited way. Moreover, pilot testing can be done through simulation software models that are readily available today. Although pilot testing may be skipped, the pros and cons of doing so should be considered. Pilot testing allows for fine-tuning improvements before going organizationwide. It also offers the chance to begin the process of tangible change within the organization earlier in the initiative. Pilot tests enable comparisons of alternative recommendations for improvement. They also provide an opportunity to achieve "quick wins," which help establish momentum for the change process. Pilot tests are also a means by which to start the process of grassroots change because they involve more people in the change process early, gaining advocates for the initiative. The greatest risk of pilot testing is that people may look at the changes as temporary because the test is limited in scope. In addition, it provides those people not included with an opportunity to stand on the sidelines and criticize the change initiative.

Feedback obtained during the pilot testing stage should be used during stage seven, when recommendations for rollout are prepared. This period should be used to develop a more "market-ready" product for the organization. For example, the pilot test may indicate that the training materials and training methods need to be revised or that the technology selected needs to be enhanced or that the measurements used to determine success need to be refined.

Once improvements are made based on information gained during the pilot tests, stage eight of the process is rollout. Grassroots change becomes paramount at this stage when the changes are rolled out and implemented in broader areas of the organization. During this stage, a roll-out schedule must be developed, materials and equipment lined up, and facilities scheduled for conducting training, announcement meetings, and so on. Options for rollout range from a multiphased process that is spread out over a period of time to a "kickoff" characterized by a short time frame when all affected areas of the organization go on-line at once.

A mistake often made is to turn the organization's attention away from the changes once implementation has been initiated and rollout is complete. However, follow-up is needed if the changes are to stick and the outcomes intended from the beginning to be realized. Stage Nine of the change process model is when grassroots change is solidified through measurement, reinforcement, and refinement. All three are key to achieving the intended results of the changes. Measurement of the desired outcomes should be made. Reinforcement should be provided to the people who embrace the change in the form of revised compensation systems, recognition by senior management, or formal and informal feedback processes. After rollout is completed, refinements should be made based on the feedback obtained. Refinements are absolutely essential to enhance the effectiveness of implemented changes and achieve the results desired.

Summary

Strategic change is characterized by the initiation of the change effort, the leadership of top management, the involvement of relatively few people within the organization, and the broad use of analytics. It is meant to result in recommendations for change and establishment of the momentum for the change effort. *Grassroots change* is characterized by the carrying forward of a change effort, the leadership of midlevel management and supervisors, and the involvement of people across and down into the organization. It is meant to result in the implementation of changes and the achievement of the desired goals of the effort.

The nine stages of the change process model described in this chapter require all management within an organization to understand and apply the characteristics of both strategic and grassroots change. The early stages of the change process model require greater application of the characteristics of strategic change. During the early stages, senior management establishes a need and develops a vision for change and a select few analyze the current organization, formulate recommendations, and detail them for testing. In contrast, the later stages of the model require a greater application of the aspects of grassroots change. More people across and down into the organization are involved during pilot testing and rollout as midlevel managers and supervisors are needed continually to measure and reinforce the changes being tested and rolled out in order to ensure successful implementation.

Figure I.3 illustrates the association between the individual stages of the change process model and the strategic and grassroots levels.

As the figure illustrates, stages one through five primarily involve the elements of strategic change. But as pointed out earlier in the chapter, involving employees through the use of surveys, interviews, or focus groups during the analysis stage (stage three) and the recommendations stage (stage four) will help begin the elements of grassroots change. Stages six through nine primarily

Figure I.3. Strategic and Grassroots
Levels of the Change Management Process Model.

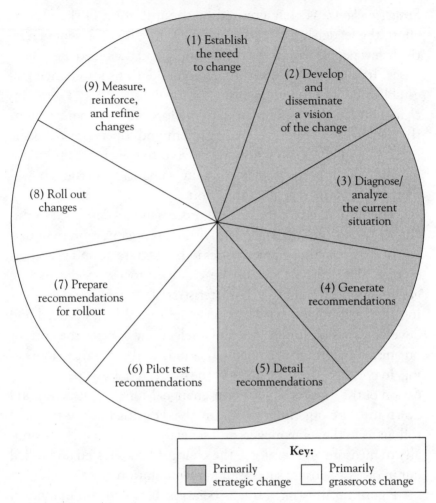

involve the elements of grassroots change because they entail implementation and reinforcement. But elements of strategic change are also required throughout these latter stages, including senior management commitment and visibility.

The chapters that follow explain how to manage the soft side of change through the nine-step model described in this introduction. The first chapters in the book—in Part One—address the strategic aspects of managing the soft side of change, which apply principally to the early stages of the model. The chapters in Part Two address the grassroots aspects of managing the soft side of change, which apply principally to the latter stages of the model. However, as already discussed, the reader should remember that in practice there is really no clear-cut delineation between the strategic and grassroots aspects of change.

Part One

At the Strategic Level

Organizationwide Change Management Imperatives

Chapter One

Teams:
Building the Infrastructure
for Effective Change

Using teams during a change effort is not a new concept. However, using them effectively can mean the difference between successful change and failure. This chapter discusses how to leverage a team infrastructure during a change process to achieve desired results most effectively.

In order to involve the greatest number of people during a process of change, improvement teams may be set up at all levels of an organization, from top management through frontline employees. Teams should be well organized and well coordinated. It is not the volume of teams that will achieve success but the effective organization and operation of them. For example, one manufacturing company began a change effort by setting up over three hundred teams across the organization. The teams were not linked in any organized way, they were not trained, and their methods of operation were haphazard. They were given only a management decree to "identify as many opportunities as possible to reduce costs." This situation only led to frustration on the part of management because little results were achieved. To make matters worse, costs actually rose in several areas of the business when managers and employees became distracted from their day to day operations. Fortunately, organizations can avert situations like this one.

Establishing a Coordinated Team Infrastructure

Besides establishing the need to change (stage one of the change process model) and developing a vision of what success will look like (stage two), building a team infrastructure to create change should be one of the first tasks management undertakes. Figure 1.1 illustrates at which stage the establishment of a team structure occurs during the nine-stage change process. (See the Introduction for a detailed discussion of the change management process model.) The figure shows that a team structure should be set up some time before stage three (diagnosis/analysis of the current situation). Management should start identifying the team structure

Figure 1.1.   The Change Management Process Model.

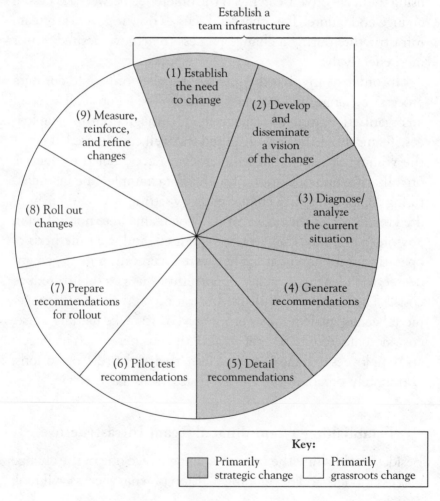

and members as early in the change process as possible. An early start is needed because team members need to be identified, notified, and made available, an effort that takes most organizations considerable time.

As a general rule, the breadth of a team structure across an organization should be determined by the breadth of the vision for change. That is, the greater the vision for change, the broader the team structure. For example, a change effort focused on one division or function—such as finance and administration—often needs only one or two teams with membership from that function. But change across an organization that involves several functions requires the establishment of teams from each area.

Figure 1.2 depicts a typical team structure for a change effort. The structure involves a steering committee, an integration team, and an improvement team assigned to each of eight areas within an organization.

Figure 1.2. A Typical Change Process Team Infrastructure.

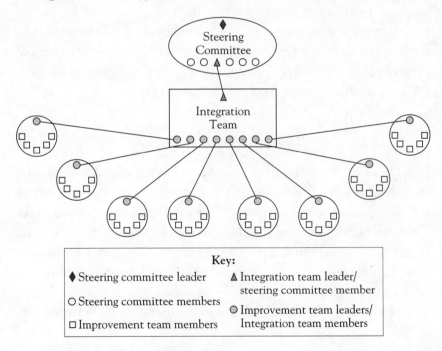

Key:

◆ Steering committee leader

○ Steering committee members

□ Improvement team members

▲ Integration team leader/
steering committee member

◉ Improvement team leaders/
Integration team members

The Steering Committee

First, it is critical to establish a team that is charged with providing direction and oversight and making key decisions essential to the progress of the change effort. This team is usually known as the steering committee. The steering committee should contain at least a few people from the organization's management who have decision-making authority but it does not have to be limited to management. A well-rounded steering committee membership includes senior management, middle management or supervisors, employees, customers, and union representatives. However, a steering committee should not be too large. Depending on the size and scope of the project, six to ten people are ideal. A group larger than ten is too unwieldy to be effective.

The steering committee should have a designated leader, identified membership, and an established role of oversight, issue resolution, and allocation or approval of resources for improvement teams. (Appendix A, Strategic Toolkit, questions 8 through 10.) Because a steering committee often includes senior members of an organization's management, it is usually not a full-time entity. Rather, the team members establish a meeting schedule to review project progress, resolve issues, and make key decisions as needed. (Appendix A, Strategic Toolkit, question 11.)

The Integration Team

In addition to the steering committee, a team charged with identifying and resolving issues across improvement teams—known as the integration team—is needed. The integration team includes the leaders from each of the improvement teams. (Improvement teams are discussed in the next sections of the chapter.) The leader of the integration team is a member of the steering committee. (See again Figure 1.2.)

In addition to addressing work items that overlap between two or more improvement teams, the integration team addresses items that are not identified by any individual team but are too important to let fall through the cracks. The team should meet about once a week during a major change effort. In addition to resolving cross-cutting issues, this weekly forum of improvement team leaders improves communication and learning among all teams. The weekly forums allow team leaders to exchange information and ideas that they can then bring back to their own teams.

Improvement Teams

Improvement teams may include four to six people (or more). One of them, the team leader, focuses on processes relating to departmental, divisional, or organizational improvements. The team members are the people who "do the work of change." That is, they conduct analyses, formulate recommendations, present recommendations to the steering committee, conduct pilot tests, refine changes for rollout, and assist with the roll-out stage of change efforts. The teams should be action oriented, results focused, and forward thinking. They should not be allowed to turn into complaint sessions or theoretical discussion groups.

Improvement teams differ from quality circles (QCs) in that QCs are ongoing departmental teams established to track progress and identify problems. Improvement teams address business processes. (Appendix A, Strategic Toolkit, question 12.) The processes assigned to a team should be an organizational priority. Figure 1.3 presents a priority matrix that can be used to rank processes identified as candidates to be worked on by improvement teams.

Unlike QCs, improvement teams have a beginning and an ending point. They may meet anywhere from a few weeks to several months or longer, depending on the scope of the change effort. But they are disbanded once improvements are implemented, refined, and working well.

Figure 1.3. Improvement Team Priority Matrix.

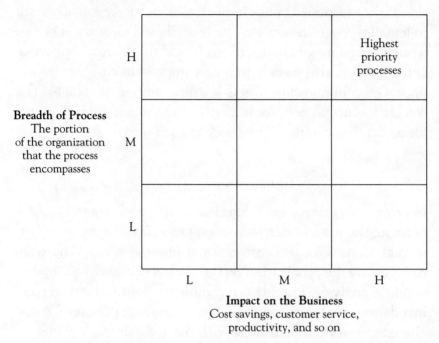

Breadth of Process
The portion
of the organization
that the process
encompasses

Impact on the Business
Cost savings, customer service,
productivity, and so on

Teams Create Better Results than Individuals

In order to be most effective, improvement teams should be bottom-line, results oriented, offering a true competitive advantage to the business. Goals should focus on increasing the value of products and services, reducing costs, or increasing customer satisfaction.

The value of high-performance employees to the success of an organizational change effort cannot be overstated. When several high-performance individuals are brought together to accomplish a task, the results are almost always greater than the combination of their individual efforts. Improvement teams take advantage of this kind of group capability by mobilizing employees to undertake all of the stages of change identified in the change process model.

Improvement teams stimulate creativity through group inter-action and participation in the change process. Improvement teams should involve people who actually do the work that is affected by the change. Broad involvement is a key element of grassroots change. Involvement in the effort leads to commitment and helps ensure the success of pilot testing and rollout. Participation does not guarantee success, but both management and employees find it far more difficult to criticize their own ideas than the ideas of others during testing and rollout.

Improvement Team Membership

The typical team includes a team leader, management, employees, ad hoc team members, and a facilitator. A team leader assures that all actions are assigned, carried out, and followed through. (Appendix A, Strategic Toolkit, question 13.) Members of improvement teams should have a working knowledge of the process being changed. However, they do not need to be experts in the entire process. Often experts see only what is, not what could be. The level of membership should vary with the scope of the team (that is, departmental, divisional, or organizational). Representatives of department, division, or organization management help bring a strategic overview of processes to a team. Employees who actually do the work being changed are invaluable for their content knowledge. Ad hoc representatives from areas of the organization that the team's actions will affect or from which the team needs help (for example, human resources, finance, systems, and so on) will assure that areas of overlap between the team's work and other areas are addressed. Besides the team leader and members, a team facilitator is needed to keep the meetings moving and on target and to ensure the participation of all team members. (Appendix A, Strategic Toolkit, question 14.) The facilitator may be an external consultant, someone from another area of the organization, or a member of the team itself. If the facilitator is a member of the team, he or she should be aware of the power within the team granted by this position and be careful not to put his or her own ideas ahead of others.

Depending on the scope of the process being addressed, participation on a team may be an individual's full-time job or an addition to a regular job. The larger the scope of the effort the more dedicated team members should be. (Appendix A, Strategic Toolkit, questions 15 and 16.) Full-time team membership for large-scale change may be illustrated by the efforts of a large oil and petrochemical company with more than sixty thousand employees around the world. The company established ten teams of from three to ten members each to work on reducing the support function costs of the organization (for example, systems, finance, human resources, purchasing, and so on). Team members were selected to work full-time for six months in one central location during the diagnosis/analysis stage of the change effort. After the initial six-month period, the ten teams were expanded into approximately thirty-five teams totaling about three hundred members working around the world for the detailing, testing, and roll-out stages of the change process.

Improvement Team Operations

Improvement teams should meet as often as deemed necessary by the team members or the steering committee, that is, every week, every day, and so on. Meetings should be focused and last as long as is needed to complete a predetermined agenda. Meetings should occur in a place where there are few or no interruptions and where there is enough room for all team members. A flip chart or white board should be available. In addition to attending team meetings, team members often have tasks that need to be completed between meetings, such as gathering information, scheduling a guest member of the team for the next meeting, and so on.

The Improvement Team Process

A team should begin its first meeting by reviewing and gaining an understanding of why it has been established, that is, it should develop a charter. If the members find that they are unclear about their charter, they should ask for more direction from the steering committee or integration team. For example, one team was put together to help "improve the store merchandise receiving process" of a retail chain. The team further clarified its objective with the steering committee by asking how it would know when the process had been sufficiently "improved." It was then able to develop a clearer objective, which was "to improve the store receiving process, from unloading to the replenishment of merchandise on the store selling floor, by reducing the cycle time by 50 percent and required people resources by 30 percent."

Once the team has been oriented and has clarified its objective, it has enough information to begin communicating with the rest of the organization (that is, explaining the objective of its work). The team's objective can be communicated through preset communication channels established for the wider change initiative that the team is a part of. Or if the team is a stand-alone entity that is not part of a broader initiative, it can begin direct communications. Whichever method used, however, beginning communication at this point is essential because open communication will help the team tap into the resources of the organization and involve others in its working process. (Methods, processes, and goals of communication are fully described in Chapter Two.)

At this point, the team begins the diagnosis/analysis stage of the change process model as it maps out the process from beginning to end and identifies problem areas, that is, areas of high cost, long cycle time, or poor quality. Mapping out the steps of a process helps team members see opportunities to improve the process by streamlining parts of it or eliminating steps altogether. During this stage, the facilitator's job is to keep the team focused on outlining the current process from beginning to end and not suggesting improvements prematurely. Team members have a tendency to want to jump right in with improvement suggestions. However, they often make early suggestions based on their own views of a piece of the process with which they regularly work. Although this may be a valuable perspective, better insight can be gained when the team looks at the entire process before making suggestions. After all members of the team see "the big picture" they are likely to generate more effective improvements or even to reinvent the process entirely rather than tinker with minor irritants.

Once the process is clearly mapped, the team begins to generate recommendations. At this stage, the team should be a free forum for flow of ideas. Idea generation is a dynamic process; it should know no boundaries. If needed, the facilitator may regularly remind the team members that at this stage they are only suggesting potential improvements. They are not making suggestions for change that will be implemented tomorrow. In reality, most ideas at this stage are never implemented. The key is to generate as many ideas as possible.

The facilitator should strive to make this a time when the team is focused on creativity. He or she must be very aware of "idea killer" statements such as "That will never work," or "That will cost too much," or "We don't have the time for that," and so on. When these or similar comments are made, the facilitator should point out that they limit the team's thinking and urge the team to open their minds to any and all ideas. One way to help establish a creative flow of ideas is to set ground rules at the start of the process. The following are ground rules that some improvement teams have found useful:

- Any idea, no matter how far-fetched, is acceptable and listed on the flip chart.
- Cost, time to implement, people needs, materials, equipment, and so on, are irrelevant at this stage.
- Team members comment on ideas only in positive ways by adding to them or expanding on them.
- No ideas may be criticized at this time; ideas will be critiqued later.
- If team members become stuck and cannot generate any ideas on one particular area, they may go on to another area of the process and return to the first topic later or during the next meeting.

Once the team has generated as many ideas as it can, the members need to revisit the list to assess the feasibility of each suggestion. Some criteria for evaluating suggestions are the following:

- Cost
- Implementation time
- People needs
- Material needs
- Equipment needs

Although these items are clearly considerations for any organization, a team should not be quick to dismiss ideas based on obstacles raised. Rather, time should be taken to address the obstacles and look for creative ways to remove, get around, or go through them. For example, in one manufacturing company, a supplier participated in funding and training, which helped reduce initial cost and skills obstacles.

After the ideas are evaluated, they should be prioritized based on both feasibility and potential positive impact. This is the time when the team should conduct an analysis that looks at the following things:

- What is the investment to implement a suggested improvement?
- What is the projected return?
- Over what time period will the return be realized?
- How will the return be measured?

After the team has narrowed down the list by prioritizing suggested improvements, it is often necessary to develop an improvement proposal in order to present suggestions to the steering committee. Unless a team has been given prior authority, most proposals generated will be submitted for review. This particularly applies to proposals that relate to capital expenditure, company policy, or matters that affect several departments or areas of the organization. The improvement proposal should be detailed enough for the steering committee members to make a go or no-go decision.

An improvement proposal should include the following information:

- Team objective
- Team members
- Current process (including process flows that describe existing pitfalls and provide metrics including costs, cycle-time, customer satisfaction, and so on)
- Proposed improvements
- Benefits of proposed improvements (cost savings, productivity gains, cycle time reductions, quality enhancements, sales increases, and so on)
- Costs of improvements
- Challenges and ways to address them (including timing, skills, available technology)
- Pilot testing and/or roll-out plan
- Supplies and equipment
- Systems support
- Training
- Physical relocation
- Labor allocation
- Timing
- Communication
- Measurements of success
- Reinforcements
- Project management responsibilities

Once the proposal is approved, the team takes the ideas into the pilot testing stage (if the changes are appropriate for testing) or directly into the rollout stage (if the changes do not lend themselves to testing). Pilot testing should not be dismissed offhand if at first it does not seem feasible. As described in the Introduction, many approaches can be taken to pilot testing, including tests of only key aspects of the changes, simulation modeling, and so on. Pilot testing helps the team during the roll-out stage.

As set out in its improvement proposal, the team needs to consider and effectively execute all aspects of the pilot testing or rollout plan. The team members must take accountability for either conducting or coordinating communication, timing, training, systems support, supplies and equipment, physical relocation, and so on. In all processes of change, challenges inevitably arise. Throughout testing or transformation, the team needs continually to monitor the progress of the changes. This will help the team address any problems that may show up and make adjustments as necessary.

Whether a pilot test is used or not, the team should have a way to measure the success of its improvements. Measurement may be made of productivity increases, cost savings, cycle time reduction, sales increases, customer satisfaction, or other outcomes. Although developing means of measurement may seem a difficult task, they are needed to assess the impact of the improvements in the areas of the organization that the team is working with and to show other management and employees who will participate in rollout in the case of a pilot test.

Team Principles

Every improvement team should be run by a set of principles or ground rules on which team members agree during their first meeting. Although the team should not spend too much time establishing the ground rules, the rules are an essential part of effective teamwork. The following are some examples of ground rules that facilitators can consider. The facilitator may propose these to the team or work the team through a process of developing its own ground rules.

1. All members of the team must be considered equal, regardless of level.

2. A strong sense of trust among team members is important to encourage participation from every member.

3. All members of the team need to openly share knowledge, concerns, and expectations.

4. Members must listen to and show respect for the views of others.

5. Members must accept the results of all decisions. However, strong dissenting opinions should be noted.

6. Every meeting should have an agenda to be optimally effective.

7. All action steps to be completed between meetings should be assigned and the date, time, and place of the next meeting set before each meeting end.

8. Notes should be kept at every meeting. All agreements and assignments of actions should be recorded.

9. All assigned actions should be carried out on schedule.

10. All relevant areas internal (departments or divisions) and external (customers and/or suppliers) to the organization should be represented on the team as appropriate.

Effective Team Facilitation

The effectiveness of any improvement team will be largely determined by the quality of the facilitator working with it. It is the facilitator's job to keep the meetings lively, productive, and focused. Good facilitation is made up of techniques that can be learned and refined through practice and coaching. The more the facilitator practices and receives feedback, the better he or she will become. Here are some helpful reminders to assist in the process:

1. Facilitators are often in a teaching role; they are there to help the group explore options for improvement.

2. Facilitators must keep the meetings moving and productive in a balance between detail and brevity.

3. The facilitator should involve all team members in the discussion and try not to let any one member of the team dominate.

4. By acknowledging the efforts of all team members, the facilitator will encourage more participation.

5. Facilitators should help ensure that all actions to happen in between meetings are distributed evenly among the team members; they must make sure one person does not have to do all the work.

6. They should keep the team focused on the objective and not let discussions wander off on tangents.

7. They must try their best to keep the flip chart neat and readable; each one is likely to be turned into meeting notes.

8. They must establish team ground rules at the start of the process, during the first meeting.

9. Facilitators should ensure that someone is keeping notes during every meeting or that someone accepts the action to turn the flip chart sheets into meeting notes.

10. They should make sure that notes from the last meeting are distributed to each team member before the next meeting.

Team Record Keeping

Good, clear meeting notes are an important part of a team's record-keeping process. Meeting notes serve several purposes. They are a record of any decisions made in a meeting. They help everyone on the team prepare for the next meeting without relying only on memories of what happened before. They can be used later to develop the improvement proposal. Finally, notes help catch up people who have missed a meeting or guest members who haven't attended earlier meetings.

Meeting notes should not be long, no more than about one to three pages if at all possible. The following is a simple and effective outline of the items that should be included to produce meeting notes.

- Meeting date
- Meeting attendees
- Meeting objective(s)
- Major discussion points
- Actions to be completed at the next meeting
- Action description
- Person who will do it
- Date action is to be completed by
- Time, date, and location of next meeting

Summary

Using a team infrastructure to accomplish a change process is a very effective way to achieve desired results. The value of each manager and employee is usually greatly enhanced when he or she works together with others in an environment that is supportive, creative, and focused on results. By effectively using a well-organized and coordinated team structure that includes a steering committee, an integration team, and improvement teams that cut across functions of the business, an organization will realize successful changes much more quickly than if individuals are asked to make changes happen on their own.

Chapter Two

Communications:
Beating the Grapevine with an
Open Two-Way Strategy

"The company is being sold."
"We are going into bankruptcy."
"There will be massive cuts."
"We are going to lose our jobs."

Unfortunately, these are familiar statements heard many times from management and employees alike. But all too often when asked where they got their information people say something like, "I heard it from Mary in the lunchroom" or "Bob told me this morning at the coffee machine." Such comments say something very important about a change effort: the grapevine has taken over. How can communications be managed effectively to beat the grapevine? Most managers at all levels believe they can do it with a memo, an announcement, or a video. But these methods are not enough. To start communicating effectively, a well thought out communications strategy is needed. The strategy should start with the process of strategic change and continue through the stages of the change process model well into the elements of grassroots change. (See Figure 2.1.)

A Framework for Organizational Communication

Luft and Ingham (1984) developed a model of interpersonal communication for programs they were conducting in group dynamics. They called their framework the *Johari Window*. Essentially, the Johari Window allows individuals to assess both how they present

Figure 2.1. The Change Management Process Model.

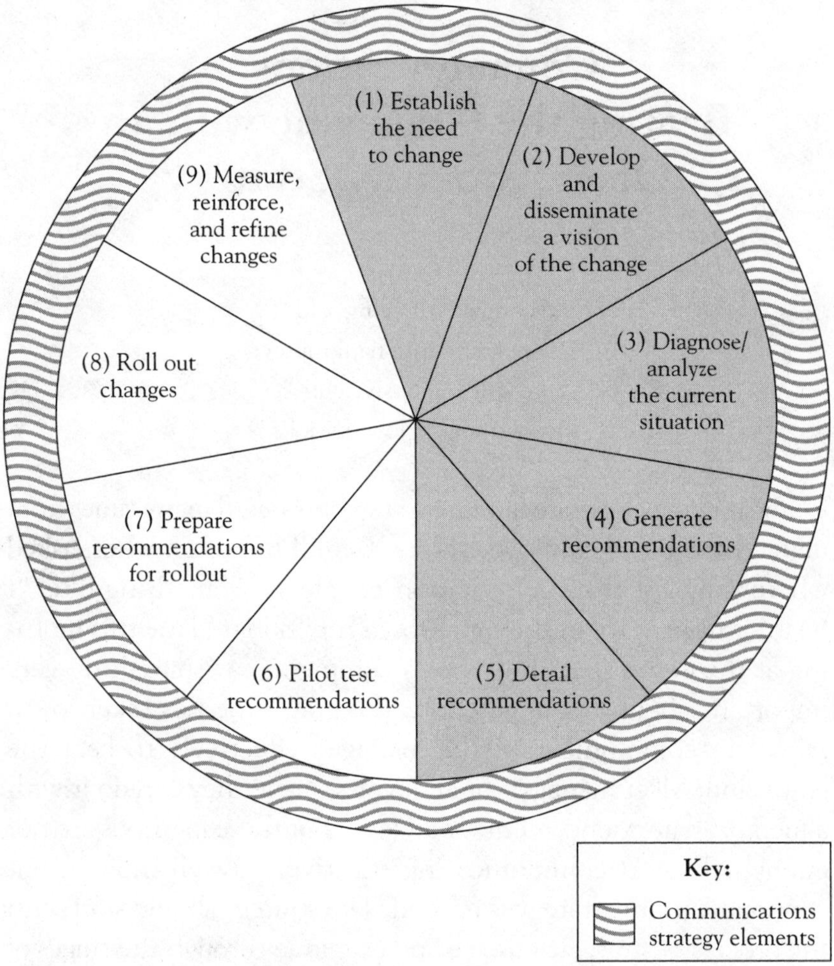

Key:

Communications strategy elements

and how they absorb the information necessary to create effective interpersonal relationships. The model uses a grid containing four regions that illustrate the amount of information exchange between individuals during interactions. The Johari Window is shown in Figure 2.2. In essence, the underlying concept of the framework is that open, two-way communications enhance interpersonal effectiveness. Taking this concept and applying it to the broader context of organizations provides a framework for understanding how organizational effectiveness can similarly be improved during a change process through an open, two-way communication process. To understand better the implications of the framework for creating effective organizational communication, we must first understand the four regions in the grid and their relationship to interpersonal effectiveness.

Region I—the arena—denotes the section of the framework that encompasses mutual understanding and shared information. The underlying concept of the Johari Window is that when information is mutually held, productivity and effectiveness in individual relationships are increased. Thus this known-by-oneself and known-by-others region is the most productive area for people to operate in. The larger the arena, the more effective, productive, and mutually beneficial a relationship becomes.

Figure 2.2. The Johari Window.

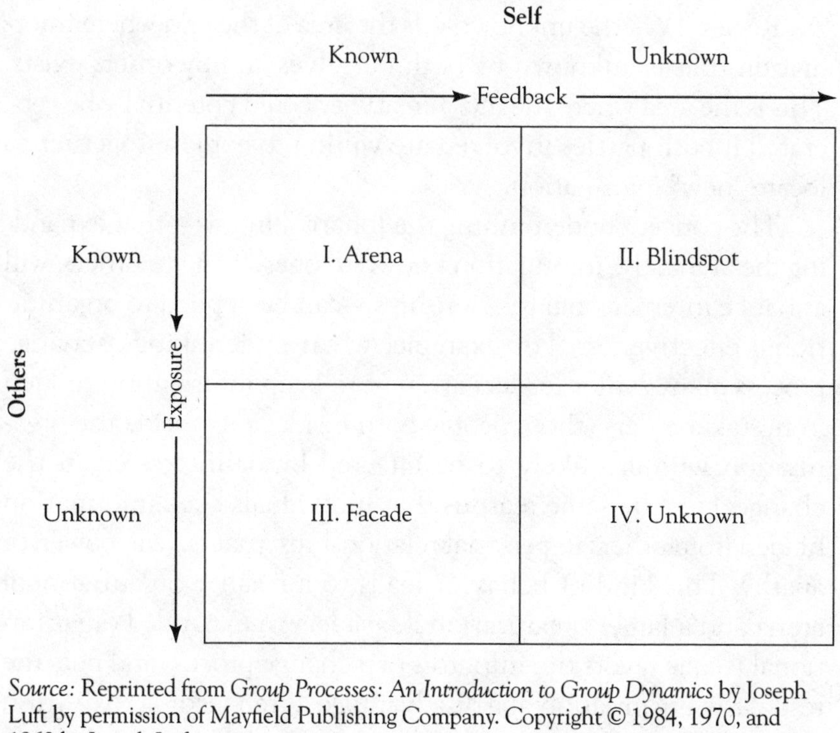

Self

		Known	Unknown
Feedback →
Known		I. Arena	II. Blindspot
Unknown		III. Facade	IV. Unknown

Others — Exposure ↓

Source: Reprinted from *Group Processes: An Introduction to Group Dynamics* by Joseph Luft by permission of Mayfield Publishing Company. Copyright © 1984, 1970, and 1963 by Joseph Luft.

Region II is the area known as the blindspot. This area of the grid represents the information that is known by others but not by oneself. The blindspot is considered to be a handicap. It is a handicap because it is unlikely we will understand the reactions and perceptions of others if we do not know the information upon which those reactions and perceptions are based. Likewise, others have an advantage over us because they know what is causing their reactions and perceptions whereas we are unaware of the cause.

Region III—the facade—is an area that hinders interpersonal effectiveness because exchange of information favors oneself. People protect themselves by hiding information. They hide information for many reasons. They may fear that the information could be used against them. Or they may have a desire for power that is characterized by keeping important information back for future use. Or they may just be apathetic; many people feel it is just too much effort to share information.

Region IV—the unknown—is the area of the grid where information that is unknown by both ourselves and by others exists. This is the area where the most creativity could potentially be generated if both parties involved are willing to explore together to locate "new" information.

The concept underpinning the Johari Window—that expanding the arena, the information known to oneself and to others, will enhance interpersonal relationships—can be applied to organizational effectiveness. For example, when undertaking a change process many senior leaders attempt to keep information hidden from stakeholders (those people both inside and outside the organization who are likely to be affected by or interested in the changes) for the same reasons that individuals keep information hidden from others in personal relationships, that is, fear, power, or apathy. This kind of behavior leads to a smaller organizational arena and a larger organizational facade. An expanded organizational facade favors the initiators of a change process and puts the rest of the organization at a disadvantage, often leading to distrust, dislike, and even acting out against the change process. Likewise, an organizational blindspot is often created when the initiators of a change process are unaware of what others in the organization are thinking, feeling, and doing in relation to the change. (See Figure 2.3.)

When transferred from interpersonal to organizational relationships, the Johari Window has key implications for enhancing a change process through improved communications. The two axes of the Johari Window—feedback and exposure—are the enablers to create more effective interpersonal interactions and more effective organizational communications. This can be done by increasing exposure by providing more information to others, thus expanding the size of the arena along the vertical axis of the grid. Likewise, by receiving and assimilating more feedback, organizations can expand the size of the arena along the horizontal axis.

A good example of the impact of the size of the organizational arena is provided through a comparison of the approaches two

Figure 2.3. The Organizational Johari Window.

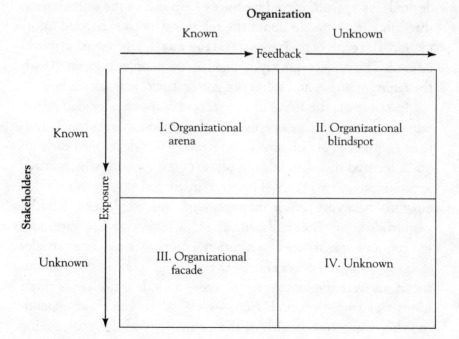

different companies took to similar change efforts. The two companies are both global organizations with over fifty thousand employees and annual sales in the multibillion dollar range. At about the same time they both began significant change efforts aimed at reducing the cost of operations.

The CEO of one of the companies made an early decision to share information about the effort with only a small senior management team. No information was formally communicated to the organization about the findings of the initiative or its progress as it developed. The CEO's comment when counseled to establish and execute a more open communication strategy was that the initial one-month diagnostic phase had gone through "like greased lightning with no one even noticing. So why should I want to communicate about this phase just to stir up trouble?" About one month into the detailed analysis phase the company was in an uproar. The teams assigned to work on the phase had to draw on the organization for needed information but could not do it in a covert way that would preserve the confidential nature of the project as the CEO desired. As a result, mixed messages went out to the organization through various teams about the reasons why they needed information, the goals of their effort, and the way the information would be used. The project quickly derailed as few people cooperated with the teams' requests and it has not gotten back on track since.

In contrast, the CEO of the second company decided at the outset to communicate openly with the organization through multiple channels. A communication strategy was developed early on and executed throughout each phase of the project, which lasted approximately two years. The strategy included face-to-face discussions between senior management and employees, lengthy worldwide conference calls with the CEO every week, continuous written messages to the organization, company newspaper articles in every issue, and other efforts. Even though some of the communications were unpleasant to receive—including notices of profit losses, reorganization, and layoffs—messages such as those explaining that the future health of the company was the goal, giving specifics about the need to change the organization, and describing what would be done for those people leaving and those staying on served to help keep the workforce motivated during the change effort.

The remainder of this chapter introduces the fundamentals, techniques, and practicalities of developing and executing a communications strategy for a change effort, whether large or small.

Communication Fundamentals

In order to be effective, a communications plan must be guided by several fundamental principles. First, messages should be linked to the strategic purpose of the change initiative. For example, if an initiative's purpose is to reduce costs, messages should explain why cost reduction is necessary, what the goal is, what the benefit of reaching the goal will be, and who will benefit from it. Clearly making the link to the strategic purpose will help establish an understanding of the need to change, keep people motivated and on track during the process of change, and establish credibility around the initiative as a positive thing to do for the business.

Second, communications should be realistic and honest. Glossing over possible negatives will create a belief that the messages are not honest. Conversely, honest communication of all aspects, both good and bad, will help people believe the messages. In addition, explaining the parameters, limits, and goals of a change effort will help prevent people from jumping to conclusions of worst case scenarios. For example, communicating that the goal of a divisional cost reduction effort is a 30 percent decrease will help preclude people from making an uninformed assumption that the entire division will be shut down.

Third, communications must be proactive rather than reactive. They should be planned in advance and begin early in the change process; they should not be offered as an afterthought or in reaction to outcries from people affected. Proactive communications will help avoid the need for a defensive position during the process. For example, let us suppose people affected by a change effort do not possess the skills necessary to take on the new responsibilities. If training is not proactively planned for these people they will become resistant to the change, complain and act out against it, and possibly refuse to take on the new responsibilities. When training programs are planned at this point, they are often inadequately designed, delivered too late to have the desired impact, and refused by those who need them.

Fourth, messages should be repeated consistently through varying channels. Just like effective advertising, a message announcing something new makes an impact through repetition and consistency. For example, an announcement about change that comes from senior management is often misinterpreted because people receive such a message through their own personal "filters," which distract them enough that they do not hear the entire message. Personal filters include thoughts about how one can avoid the change, a focus on personal disagreement with certain aspects of the change, or questions about how the change will affect one's own situation. But multiple, consistent messages enable people to internalize the message and more clearly hear all components of it. Using multiple channels of communication increases the opportunity for people to receive the whole message and to internalize it. Channels used can include announcements from management, videos, memos, newsletters, and small group meetings.

Finally, avenues of two-way communication are needed to help ensure successful implementation of the changes, that is, feedback mechanisms must be established. Feedback should occur during the design, testing, and roll-out phases. Effective feedback mechanisms should focus on four elements. During the design phase, they should focus on the concerns of the stakeholders. After implementation begins, they should focus on what is working well and what needs to be refined. During rollout, they should seek to determine whether the goals of the change are being achieved, that is, cost reductions, cycle time reductions, service improvement, and so on. And after rollout, they should look for lessons learned that can be applied to conducting future change initiatives more effectively. Feedback is thus the key element in creating an organization that learns from what it does.

Avoiding Common Pitfalls

Several lessons may be learned from the communication pitfalls that occur during a change process. Communication mistakes are often exposed during a period of change as symptoms of poor management of the process. The first common trap is believing that by keeping information close to the vest, management, employees, and those external to the organization will learn about the effort only from official communication vehicles. Not true! The grapevine is always active and quick. Examples occur daily: even the best-kept secrets of business and government are speculated about and reported on in the media. To avoid this pitfall, a communications strategy must be formulated and initiated as early as possible.

Another common mistake is to delegate communications to a communications department. A communications department can be useful in assisting with message formulation, identifying and setting up delivery channels, and helping to execute established communication events. However, ownership of the messages of the change process must be claimed by management. When management attempts to delegate ownership it sends a strong message to the organization that the change is not important enough for management to devote its time to it. People interpret this message as a lack of management commitment and as a result frequently will not commit to the change themselves.

Another mistake is to provide a poor description of the change during the communication process. Key aspects of the change are often glossed over, including the genesis of the change, the sequence of the events that will be taking place, and the people who will be involved. Inadequate description of change often results in implementation breaking down at lower levels and employees questioning management's knowledge of the details.

A fourth pitfall lies in a poor communication process or plan, often the result when little priority is given to the communication process. A poor communication process or plan will result in unclear definition of roles and insufficient follow-up or fine-tuning once implementation begins. Conversely, a carefully designed and executed communications plan serves as an effective vehicle to break down barriers to change and establish buy in.

Fifth, insufficient communication from senior leaders will often result in middle management killing initiatives and changes being seen as temporary or reversible. The commitment of senior management must be shown throughout the communication process in order to send a message to the organization that the changes are an organizational priority. Senior management priorities are communicated not only by what is said but also by what is done. Taking the time to make announcements and conduct question and answer sessions will show the organization the importance of the initiatives to senior management.

A sixth key mistake is to shut down communications channels once changes have been developed and are being rolled out. This often happens because by this stage management has usually reconciled whatever its concerns may have been because of immersion in the development and direction setting of the change. Yet this is often the time when even more open communication is needed by the people at the lower levels of the organization. During rollout, people will have questions they want answered, concerns they want heard, and suggestions they think will make changes work better. All of these issues can be addressed by keeping open the communications channels that should have been established early in the process, including announcements, written communications, and feedback sessions between employees and management.

Communication Helps Lower Resistance

Possibly the most important pitfall to any change process is not understanding resistance to change. As discussed in the Introduc-

tion, resistance is likely to be encountered at all levels of an organization. Lack of understanding of it often results at best in frustration and at worst in dysfunctional behavior, that is, acting out
against the change, the initiators of the change, and the organization itself. Understanding the reasons for resistance and working
with it rather than against it will aid greatly in creating a smoother
process of change. Understanding resistance will also help to
develop a well thought out communications plan. Figure 2.4 shows
the resistance pyramid, a framework for understanding the reasons
why people resist change.

The design of the resistance pyramid is based upon the resistance hierarchy developed by Nieder and Zimmerman at the
University of Bremen, Germany. Like Maslow's hierarchy of needs,
the resistance pyramid is a succession of levels, in this case resistance levels. Satisfaction at each level of resistance reduces resistance at the next level. For example, when we respond to people's
need to know, they become more open to learning the new skills
and abilities involved in changing. And once they have the new
skills, they will gain the confidence to overcome unwillingness to
change.

Based on the resistance pyramid concept, what people need

Figure 2.4. The Resistance Pyramid.

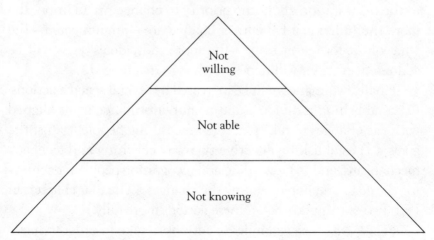

first is knowledge. Knowledge can be provided through information about the change process. The information should be based upon what management and employees want to know. People usually want the basic questions answered: What is happening? Why are we doing this? How will it take place? When will it happen? And who will it affect? Answering these questions for people at each phase of a change process will help them move up to the next level of the pyramid.

The second level of the pyramid—ability—is addressed through training and education. In order to change, people are likely to need new skills. New skills for employees may include operating new equipment or systems, working in teams rather than as individuals, or following revised procedures. Management often need new skills to create teams and foster teamwork, coach employees to provide them with new skills, and apply new procedures. Because ability has a profound impact on the willingness that people have to undertake new activities and make changes, training becomes an integral part of communication and the change process.

The top level of the pyramid is willingness. The acquisition of knowledge at the lowest level and new skills at the middle level will help people become more willing to change. However, other factors should be addressed as well. As discussed earlier, the involvement of senior management in the communication process will send signals to the organization about the priority to change. In addition, the more the individual benefits of change are communicated—the what's-in-it-for-me message—the more individuals' egos will be addressed and their willingness to change encouraged.

Finally, willingness can be increased by several specific actions: (1) establishing individual and team performance goals aligned with the changes to take place, (2) measuring people against the goals, (3) establishing effective two-way coaching and feedback mechanisms, and (4) rewarding and recognizing people for achieving the goals and implementing the changes. (The four chapters in Part Two of this book detail these actions more fully.)

Figure 2.5 offers examples of actions to take in order to move people up the resistance pyramid.

Figure 2.5. Actions to Take to Overcome Resistance.

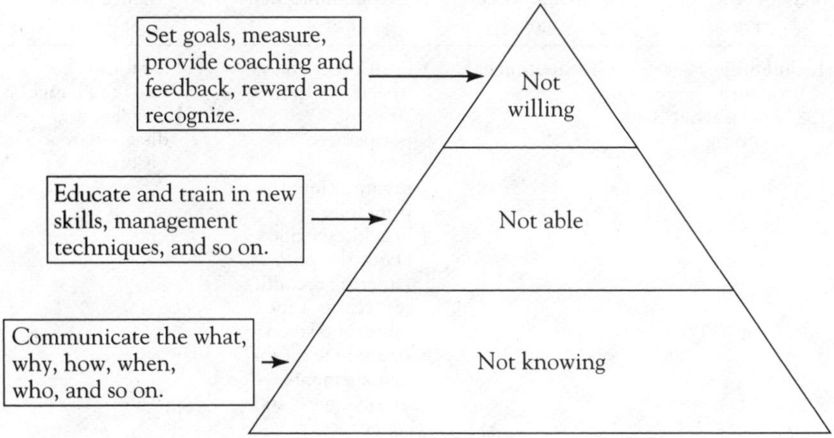

Set goals, measure, provide coaching and feedback, reward and recognize. → Not willing

Educate and train in new skills, management techniques, and so on. → Not able

Communicate the what, why, how, when, who, and so on. → Not knowing

Phases of the Communication Process

The purpose of communication shifts as a change initiative takes shape. For example, early in the process the focus of communication is on announcing to the organization what is happening and what the process will entail. But as the process moves along, the focus shifts to the "big picture," to provide an overview of the changes being developed and identify issues that exist or may arise. Any pilot tests being conducted should be monitored, with lessons learned gathered and woven into the communications for rollout. During rollout, communications must become more specific and center on implications for various parts of the organization and the individuals within it. Communication during rollout also involves skill acquisition, including training in new skills, roles, and methods. Finally, during implementation communications shift to emphasize refinement. Refinement means listening to and acting upon management and employee feedback about how to adjust the changes to obtain the desired outcomes. Table 2.1 illustrates the four communication phases of a change effort. The table also identifies the scope of communication during each phase, the purpose of each phase, and the relationship between each phase of communication with the nine stages of the change process model presented in Chapter One.

Table 2.1. The Four Communication Phases of a Change Effort.

Communication Phase	Communication Scope	Communication Purpose	Change Model Stage(s)
1. Building awareness ("This is what is happening.")	Organizationwide	• Position change initiatives from a strategic perspective • Reaffirm organizational principles • Provide specifics about the process (steering committee, teams, timetable, and so on) • Announce senior management involvement and support	(1) Establish the need to change (2) Develop and disseminate a vision
2. Giving project status ("This is where we are going.")	Organization-specific	• Demonstrate senior management commitment • Reaffirm strategic rationale • Identify management and employee issues • Gain information from pilot tests • Provide the big picture for change blueprints	(3) Diagnose/analyze the current situation (4) Generate recommendations (5) Detail recommendations (6) Pilot test recommendations (7) Prepare recommendations for roll out
3. Rolling out ("This is what it means to you.")	Project-specific	• Continue to show senior management commitment • Provide specifics on the changes being made • Share implications of change with those affected • Provide training for new roles, skills, methods	(8) Roll out
4. Following up ("This is how we will make it work.")	Team-specific	• Continue to show senior management commitment • Reaffirm organizational principles and strategic focus • Listen to and act on feedback to make changes successful • Refine changes to ensure success	(9) Measure, reinforce, and refine

Although the communication process evolves as the change initiative takes shape, there are some constants throughout all phases. The most important of these is demonstration of senior management support for the change initiatives. As discussed earlier in this chapter, senior management must take the time to communicate during all phases of the process. The weight of its input and interaction will have a tremendous effect on the acceptance of change within the organization.

Another important constant throughout the process is keeping people aware of how the changes fit into the organization's principles and strategic focus. Doing this will help people see the changes within the context of future organizational success.

Specifics

Once the phases of the communication process are understood, a specific strategy for communication at each phase must be developed. The communication strategy matrix shown in Table 2.2 provides a structured, pragmatic approach to developing a specific communications plan for any change effort. (Appendix A, Strategic Toolkit, questions 17 to 22.)

The first step in the matrix is identifying key stakeholders, the people both internal and external to the organization who must be communicated with. (Appendix A, Strategic Toolkit, question 17.) As explained earlier, stakeholders are those people who are likely to be affected by or have an interest in the changes. Such people include senior management, middle management, employees, customers, suppliers, shareholders, and the community in which the organization resides. Once stakeholders have been identified, their stake in the change must be identified, that is, their interest in it must be defined. The question most people want answered is, "What's in it for me?" Once this question has been answered for them, the stakeholders will be more willing to hear about the broader issues, such as the benefits to the company as a whole (including competitive advantages or increased market share). Employees will want to know if they will lose their jobs,

Table 2.2. Communications Strategy Matrix.

| | | | *Example for Phase 3: Rollout* | | | |
Stakeholders	Objectives	Key Messages	Vehicles	Timing	Accountability
Middle Management	• Buy in • Understanding • New skills	• New roles • New methods • Personal impact	• Meetings with CEO/executives • Training	• Kickoff/week 1 • Kickoff/month 1	• CEO/executives • Training department
Employees	• Buy in • Understanding • New skills	• New methods • New skills • Personal impact	• Meetings with managers • Training	• Kickoff/week 1 • Kickoff/month 1	• Managers • Training department/ managers
Customers	• Information • Awareness	• New methods • Service impact	• Meetings with sales representatives	• Kickoff/week 1	• Sales representatives
Shareholders	• Information • Awareness	• Service impact • Financial impact	• Written information from CEO/CFO	• Kickoff/week 1	• CEO/and CFO
Community	• Information • Awareness	• Service impact • Financial impact	• News release	• Kickoff/week 1	• CEO

how their work will be affected, if they will have to relocate, and so on. Middle management will want answers to these same questions. Middle managers will also want to know other things, such as if they will continue to manage the same people or report to the same boss. Shareholders will also have the obvious questions, including how the change will affect the company's profits and if it will establish competitive advantage or increase market share. Members of the communities in which the organization is present will want to know whether there will be a loss of jobs (which would negatively affect local businesses), whether the organization is planning to move, and whether there will be a need for new employees in the future. Suppliers will want to know if their orders will be cut or if they will need to step up production to meet increased demand. These kinds of questions, which will weigh heavily on the minds of the stakeholders, should be addressed early. If they are not, the grapevine will provide its own answers for each group and often they will not be the answers the organization intends them to receive.

Once the key stakeholders have been identified, the objectives sought to be achieved by communicating them must be determined. (Appendix A, Strategic Toolkit, question 18.) For instance, in order to help ensure that changes are made successfully and will last, buy in—willingness—must be established among several constituencies. Establishing buy in is a very different matter from merely informing about the changes to take place. Using the resistance pyramid as a guide, the first steps in building buy in are to inform people about the changes (provide them with knowledge) and to educate them (increase their ability). Accomplishing these two steps will help greatly in the effort to establish willingness, the top level of the pyramid.

Third, key messages or the content of the communication that will achieve the objectives of communication efforts must be developed. (Appendix A, Strategic Toolkit, question 19.) Key messages may include the new roles of people affected by the changes, the reasons for the changes, and the benefits of the changes for individuals, the organization, customers, and shareholders. Benefits mentioned may include improved service to customers, decreased cycle time, better financial performance, and so on. Furthermore, when the purpose of communication, in the form of training, is to develop new skills and abilities within the organization, the how to's or training objectives become the key messages of the effort.

Fourth, the vehicles that will be used to communicate the key messages should be identified. (Appendix A, Strategic Toolkit, question 20.) Several means of communication should be used to repeat continually the messages that need to be sent. Communication vehicles may include memos, speeches, large and small group meetings of employees and management, videos, newsletters, electronic message boards, training sessions and workshops, news releases, posters, and others. Using various communication vehicles and channels will help stakeholders "hear" messages better.

Fifth, the timing of the communications must be determined. (Appendix A, Strategic Toolkit, question 21.) Timing refers to both when communication will happen and how often it will happen. It is important to keep one factor in mind when developing the timing: messages are most effective when they are consistent and repetitive. Consistency helps establish the credibility of the messages. Repetition helps people see the importance of the messages and the importance of the changes the messages are communicating.

Sixth, accountability for both delivering and making the communications happen needs to be determined. (Appendix A, Strategic Toolkit, question 22.) The people who will deliver the communication need to be identified. They may include senior management, middle management, trainers, employees, and any others needed. People who will make the communication occur should also be identified. For example, if a senior executive is slated to participate in a meeting with employees, someone in the organization may be designated to schedule the meeting, draft an outline or agenda, and brief the executive before the meeting. If a newsletter will be used as a regular communication vehicle, someone will have to pull the contents together, edit it, make sure it gets printed, and see that it is distributed to everyone who should receive it. Without accountability being designated for each communication action, invariably something will fall through the cracks.

Finally, experience proves time and again that all changes need refinement during implementation. Refinement is accomplished through the use of feedback mechanisms once initial changes are kicked off. (Appendix A, Strategic Toolkit, questions 23 to 26.) For example, during the roll-out stage, one company set up a special team of two people whose sole role was to gather feedback from parts of the organization implementing changes. They received feedback through electronic mail, focus groups, and a telephone hot line that employees and management called to point out adjustments needed in their area. The team then channeled the information to the appropriate senior managers for action.

Whether a special team is used to collect feedback or not, the main focus should be on establishing a mechanism to listen to and act upon management and employee feedback about adjustments needed. Doing this will help ensure that the changes being rolled out will achieve the desired outcomes.

Summary

The Johari Window framework suggests that to enhance organizational communication during a change process organizations need to expand the organizational arena. This can be done in two key ways: by providing more information to the stakeholders in the change and by soliciting and assimilating more feedback from the stakeholders. In addition, using communication fundamentals helps to work with resistance rather than against it. Communication fundamentals include linking messages to the strategic purpose of the change, being realistic and honest in communications, taking a proactive rather than reactive approach, and delivering consistent and repeated messages through multiple channels.

Even when these fundamentals are adhered to, rumor and hearsay will never be totally eliminated. However, applying these concepts to develop and implement a well thought out communications strategy throughout all the stages of a change effort will ultimately help beat the grapevine.

Chapter Three

Culture:
Managing All the Components

Implementing and, especially, sustaining the goals of organizational change efforts have proven to be difficult at best and impossible at worst for many organizations. Most change initiatives fall short of reaching their goals when "the rubber hits the road," that is, during implementation and follow up. The change process frequently focuses on the tangible changes—changes in operations, systems, and procedures—which are the easiest to identify. But effective implementation mandates that all changes be clearly connected to an organization's culture. Making this connection not only enables effective implementation but also embeds change into the daily life of an organization. As a result, change is sustained and desired effects—such as lower costs, increased revenue, improved customer service, fewer errors, reduced cycle times—are achieved.

Making the connection between culture and change requires a systematic approach. Proposed changes should be passed through a "cultural screen" that identifies how best to implement and embed changes into an organization. This chapter presents a pragmatic approach to linking organizational culture to the change process to help effectively implement and sustain the recommended changes.

Operationalizing Organizational Culture

Components of culture can be isolated but no one component fully characterizes an organizational culture. Instead, organizational culture is a blend of interrelated elements. As individual components interact each day within an organization they collectively create that organization's culture. For example, one manager who continually commands her subordinates may be called authoritarian. But her leadership style does not mean that the organization's overall culture is authoritarian. In fact, many other managers in the same organization may frequently solicit input from employees during decision-making processes. As a result, the managers in the organization collectively contribute to a participative culture.

Table 3.1 illustrates ten components that together establish an operational description of organizational culture. By identifying discernible components of organizational culture we can determine the tangible elements that may be managed to help implement and sustain change. However, just as no single component of the ten identified in the table defines culture, it will not suffice to involve only one in support of a desired change.

Managing Organizational Culture During Change

The primary function of culture management during a process of change is to implement and sustain changes. Too often executives and managers struggle to implement changes because they lack an understanding of how to make the changes important to employees. For example, a large retailer identified customer service as a major obstacle to revenue growth. In particular, the service behavior of employees did not compare favorably with the competition. The service they were providing was not bad, but an analysis of

Table 3.1. An Organization's Cultural Components.

Cultural Components	
Rules and policies	Management behaviors
Goals and measurement	Rewards and recognition
Customs and norms	Communications
Training	Physical environment
Ceremonies and events	Organizational structure

what the competition was offering and what customers wanted indicated that the competitors were moving well ahead in the area of customer service. In an effort to improve the situation, management declared that excellence in customer service was important and that poor service "would not be tolerated." In addition, the company spent a significant amount of resources (both capital and time) to train employees in new service behaviors. Unfortunately, these two actions were not enough to implement the desired changes in service behaviors and make the new behaviors stick. After a brief increase in service ratings upon completion of the training, the ratings quickly fell off again.

This example illustrates how managing only one or two aspects of an organization's culture will not effectively implement or sustain change. In this case two of the elements listed in Table 3.1 were targeted: training and communications. How could the company have done better? It should have embedded service excellence into the culture of the organization by managing *as many of the ten components as possible*. In order to choose which of the components in Table 3.1 to use to implement and sustain change, desired changes need to be sent through a cultural screen. Doing so will identify all of the elements of organizational culture that can be leveraged to implement and sustain change successfully.

Applying a Cultural Screen

The ten components listed in Table 3.1 together can be applied to the change process as a cultural screen, as indicated in Figure 3.1.

All ten of the cultural screen components in Figure 3.1 are not always applicable to make every recommended change happen. Rather, every identified change should be "screened" in order to select the cultural aspects that a company can leverage to implement and sustain it. (Appendix A, Strategic Toolkit, question 27.) Cultural screening should occur during stage five of the change process model, when recommendations are detailed. (See Figure 3.2.)

Figure 3.1. The Cultural Screen.

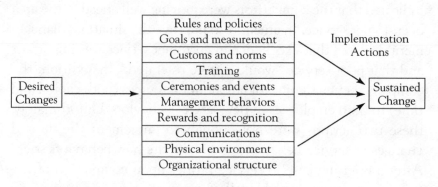

The best way to apply the screening process is first to choose a recommended change, for example, the implementation of a new financial system. The second step is to identify any aspect of implementing the change that is associated with any of the ten cultural components shown in Figure 3.1. For example, are any aspects of the company's rules and policies, goals and measurement, customs and norms, training, ceremonies and events, management behaviors, rewards and recognition, communications, physical environment, or organizational structure associated with the implementation of the new financial system? In this case, the answer may be *yes* to all ten questions. Old rules and policies will need to be replaced by new rules and policies that reinforce the new system's procedures. Management and employees will need new goals and measurements that support using the new system. Customs and norms—such as using financial reports created by the old system—will need to be replaced by the new norm of using information from reports made available by the new system. This type of screening process should continue down the list of all ten cultural components.

Putting a desired change through this screening process enables organizations to identify the cultural components that will facilitate implementing and sustaining desired changes. For example, a large manufacturing company wanted to implement a new purchasing process that would result in lower costs and more accurate

Figure 3.2. The Change Management Process Model.

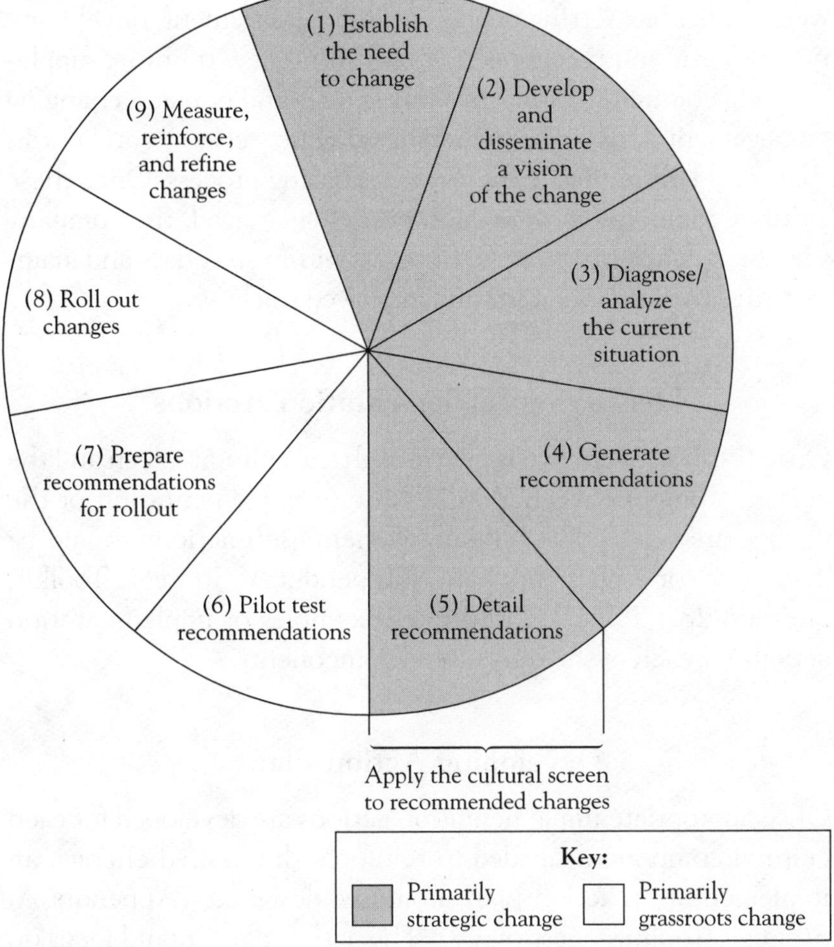

(1) Establish the need to change

(2) Develop and disseminate a vision of the change

(3) Diagnose/analyze the current situation

(4) Generate recommendations

(5) Detail recommendations

(6) Pilot test recommendations

(7) Prepare recommendations for rollout

(8) Roll out changes

(9) Measure, reinforce, and refine changes

Apply the cultural screen to recommended changes

Key:
Primarily strategic change   Primarily grassroots change

tracking. At first glance, implementation did not appear to be all that complex. The new process was easy to understand and "looked good on paper." Yet when presented with the new purchasing process the employees involved were not eager to make the required changes. When explored in greater depth from an implementation perspective, management realized that the old process was still being reinforced by the old training, goals and measurement, management behaviors, and so on. So the company decided to apply the cultural screen to the implementation of the process changes. As a result, it was found that seven cultural components were applicable: setting new goals and measurement, developing new rewards and recognition, establishing new training, supplementing communications, redefining rules and policies, changing management behaviors, and establishing new customs and norms that would all reinforce the new purchasing process. Once these cultural components were appropriately managed, the company was able to implement the new process within sixty days and maintain the goals of lower costs and improved tracking.

Identifying Implementation Actions

Once the desired change is put through the cultural screen and the cultural components that will facilitate implementation of the change are selected, specific implementation actions should be developed for each component. (Appendix A, Strategic Toolkit, question 28.) Table 3.2 illustrates examples of implementation actions for each of the ten cultural components.

Developing Action Plans

Once appropriate implementation actions are developed for each cultural component needed to reinforce the desired change, an implementation action plan should be designed. (Appendix A, Strategic Toolkit, question 29.) The action plan should focus on successfully leveraging each cultural component to implement and sustain the desired changes. The plan should include the people involved, the timing of implementation, and the resources needed. Table 3.3 illustrates an action plan for the management behaviors component that will support the use of a new order entry system.

Implementing the Actions

Once a viable action plan is developed for each cultural component involved, all action plans need to be implemented. To implement

Table 3.2. Implementation Actions.

Cultural Components	Example Implementation Actions
Rules and policies	• Eliminate rules and policies that will hinder performance of new methods and procedures. • Create new rules and policies that reinforce the desired ways of operating. • Develop and document new Standard Operating Procedures (SOPs).
Goals and measurement	• Develop goals and measurements that reinforce the desired changes. • Make goals specific to operations (establish procedural goals and measures for employees who conduct the process being changed rather than financial goals that are a by-product of the change, which employees cannot easily relate actions to).
Customs and norms	• Eliminate old customs and norms that reinforce the old ways of doing things and replace with new customs and norms that reinforce the new ways (replace written memos with face to face weekly meetings).
Training	• Eliminate training that reinforces the old way of operating and replace with training that reinforces the new. • Deliver training just in time so people can apply it immediately (schedule training to occur just before employees and managers need to apply new skills and techniques). • Develop experiential training that provides real-time, hands-on experience with new procedures.
Ceremonies and events	• Establish ceremonies and events to reinforce the new ways (conduct awards ceremonies for teams that achieve set goals, hold recognition events that highlight employees and managers who successfully implement changes).
Management behaviors	• Develop goals and measurements that reinforce the desired management behaviors. • Provide training to management that focuses on the new behaviors.

Table 3.2. Implementation Actions, Cont'd.

Cultural Components	*Example Implementation Actions*
	• Publicly recognize and reward managers who change to the desired behaviors (link promotion and pay rewards to the desired behaviors). • Penalize managers who do not change behaviors (do not give promotions, pay increases, or bonuses to those who do not demonstrate the desired behaviors).
Rewards and recognition	• Eliminate the old rewards that reinforce the old ways and replace them with new rewards that reinforce the new ways. • Make it clear that rewards and recognition are for making changes happen (make rewards specific to the change goals that have been set).
Communications	• Eliminate communication that reinforces the old way of operating and replace it with communication that reinforces the new. • Deliver communication in new ways to show commitment to the changes (use multiple channels to deliver consistent messages before, during, and after the changes are made). • Make communications two-way (solicit regular feedback from management and employees about the changes being made).
Physical environment	• Establish a physical environment that reinforces the changes (colocate management and employees who will need to work together to make changes successful, use "virtual offices" to encourage people to work outside the office with customers, use telecommunications to connect people who need to interact across geographies).
Organizational structure	• Establish an organizational structure that will reinforce operational changes (set up client service teams, eliminate management layers, centralize or decentralize work as needed, combine overlapping divisions).

Table 3.3. Management Behaviors Implementation Action Plan for New Order Entry System.

Actions	People Involved	Timing	Resources Needed
• Development, announcement, and implementation of goals, measurement, and rewards for management who learn to use the new system • Measurement and reward of managers who train and reinforce their employees to use the new order entry system and procedures	• Executives to approve goals, measurement, and rewards • Three- to four-person team to design measurement and rewards criteria • Line management to use the new systems and procedures • Executives to approve measures and rewards • Three- to four-person team to design measurement and rewards criteria (same as above) • Line management to be responsible for developing employee skills	• Development and approval of goals, measures, and rewards by kickoff date • Rewards given within 90 days of kickoff • Development and approval of measures and rewards by kickoff date • Rewards given within 90 days of kickoff	• Three- to four-person design team • Approved rewards (monetary other) • Three- to four-person design team (same as above) • Approved rewards (monetary or other)

them effectively, all the resources, people, and timing delineated in the plans must be adhered to. (Appendix A, Strategic Toolkit, question 30.) Not doing this will send strong messages to the organization that management is not serious about changing the organization and the commitment needed to implement and sustain change will be lost. For example, a large chemical company wanted to implement changes in several of its human resources (HR) processes (recruiting, performance management, and salary administration) by turning over most of the activities involved to management and employees instead of using the HR professionals in the organization to perform them. The company began the initiative by following the change process management model. First, the activities to be performed by management and employees were identified. These changes were then run through the cultural screen. Eight cultural components that would be used to facilitate implementing and sustaining the changes were identified: rules and policies, goals and measurements, customs and norms, training, ceremonies and events, management behaviors, rewards and recognition, and communications. Next, action plans were developed for each of the eight components. However, when the action plans were implemented a series of events took place that demonstrated to management and employees alike that the company was not serious about making the changes. Training schedules slipped. Senior managers did not show up for rewards events. Events were canceled. Little of the communication that was planned actually occurred. As a result, implementation went poorly and the desired changes to the HR processes were never made.

Measuring the Impact

After the action plans are started and implementation has begun, the impact of making the changes should be measured. There are two primary reasons for doing this. First of all, an organization must be able to determine when goals for change have been achieved. Has there been a decline in absenteeism, an improvement in customer service, a reduction in cost, an enhancement of teamwork? Without reliable measurement these questions cannot be credibly answered; organizations would only be guessing. Measurement removes the guesswork. Secondly, measurement provides a way to track progress. When a company determines what to measure and how to measure it, it can see whether the organization is on the way to achieving its change goals. The accomplishment of goals shouldn't come as a surprise. Periodic measurement allows people to see what progress is being made toward change goals. Management and employees alike can observe progress as they achieve implementation milestones. Intermediate landmarks help people stay motivated and keeps them committed to achieving the final goals of change.

A complete picture of the effectiveness of changes made can be obtained through a combination of quantitative and qualitative measures. (Appendix A, Strategic Toolkit, question 31.) Measures of effectiveness that go beyond financial performance include behavioral observation of employees and management. For example, behaviors can be counted, described, and summarized to draw conclusions about the changes made, such as customer service improvement, teamwork enhancement, or communications improvement. In addition to behavioral observation, management and employee feedback can help determine the impact of the changes made. Management and employees are often the best sources for answers to such questions as the following: Was there a shift in perceptions about job satisfaction? What is working well or not so well regarding the changes made? What is the impact of the changes on customers? In addition, organizational innovation may be indicated by the time it takes to develop new products and services or the number of new products developed in a year. As with any measurement fundamental steps need to be taken, including assigning accountability to gather the information, establishing methods of data collection, setting the frequency of collection, using sound data analysis techniques, and creating useful reporting formats. (Measurement will be discussed more fully in Chapter Six.)

Continuing to Manage Cultural Components to Reinforce Change

To ensure that change goals are achieved once implementation and measurement have both started, the cultural components should continue to be managed. (Appendix A, Strategic Toolkit, question 32.) Continued management of the cultural components during a change effort is essential to reinforce and embed change into the daily operations of the organization. For example, as a major retailer implemented changes to the stock replenishment process, management and employee feedback indicated that there was still a need to improve the communication between merchandise buyers and the stores. This finding prompted further action to reinforce communication. Buyers were moved into store locations so they could target their purchases to local markets.

In contrast, when organizations "take their eyes off the ball" after changes begin to be made, implementation efforts slip. Change that is not continually managed will not yield sustained results. One company's efforts to implement changes to its sales process in order to increase sales volume serves as an example. The company offered excellent training for all employees involved, provided frequent communication through multiple channels, and realigned goals, measurement, and rewards and recognition with the desired changes. However, once the new sales process was kicked off and initial results were achieved—with an increase of ten percentage points across all regions—management stopped managing the process, dropping the use of measures and rewards. The result? The goals achieved within the first two months after kickoff were short-lived and after six months performance returned to before-implementation levels.

Continuing management of the cultural aspects of a change effort reinforces the operational, technical, and procedural changes being made. It helps to ensure that the changes made last. The procedure for ongoing management of the cultural aspects should be built into the implementation action plan described earlier in this chapter. First, an "ongoing section" of the action plan should identify who will be responsible for continuing management of the cultural components—for example, who will continue to train newly hired employees to use redesigned procedures, who will update rules and policies as needed, who will continue to organize the ceremonies and events used to recognize employees who are successful at implementing the desired changes, and so on. The ongoing section of the plan should also identify the time frame for continuing management. For example, should rewards and recognition continue indefinitely or should they stop after a defined period of time once the changes are in place? Finally, the ongoing section of the action plan should identify the resources needed to continue to manage cultural components, for example, training facilities to continue education, budgets to continue communications, and individuals to update regularly the goals and measurements and rules and policies of the changes made.

Summary

The most difficult aspect to manage in any organizational change effort is arguably that of cultural change. Furthermore, because culture seems so difficult to manage, many organizations just ignore it and focus instead on the more tangible aspects of change, such as operations, equipment, systems, and procedures. But achieving and sustaining the goals of organizational change efforts mandate that the culture of an organization be involved. Applying a cultural screen like the one described in this chapter will help facilitate implementation of the change process. An organization committed to changing its operations, systems, procedures, and the like must work on as many of the ten cultural issues in the screen as possible. In order to do so, it must develop comprehensive action plans for each applicable cultural component, implement the action plans rigorously, measure the impact of the changes, and continue to manage the cultural components. Performing these steps before, during, and after implementation of desired changes will help create lasting operational and cultural change.

Chapter Four

Leadership:
Developing the Key Attributes
for Leading Change

Many day-to-day aspects of a change effort can be delegated, including gathering information for analysis, developing ideas for new methods and procedures, and designing training materials for pilot testing and rollout. However, leadership of a change effort cannot be delegated. To ensure the success of an organizational change effort, the key people in an organization—from top-level executives to frontline supervisors—must lead the change process with commitment and skill. The commitment to leading a change initiative ultimately comes from within each individual. Although managers may be offered incentives such as monetary rewards, perks, or stock options, they must choose personally to do what is needed in order to lead a change initiative. Once they are committed to making a change effort successful, managers must acquire and use the attributes they need to make the changes happen. That is, they must change their own behaviors. The behavioral aspect of leading a change initiative is one of the most difficult to achieve. Yet effective leadership is a critical element of strategic change.

This chapter describes the attributes change leaders must develop and proposes a model for developing leadership behaviors in order to acquire these attributes. The process of developing change leadership attributes and skills should start at the beginning of strategic change and be ongoing, lasting through all stages of the change management process model and throughout the elements of grassroots change. (See Figure 4.1.)

Figure 4.1. The Change Management Process Model.

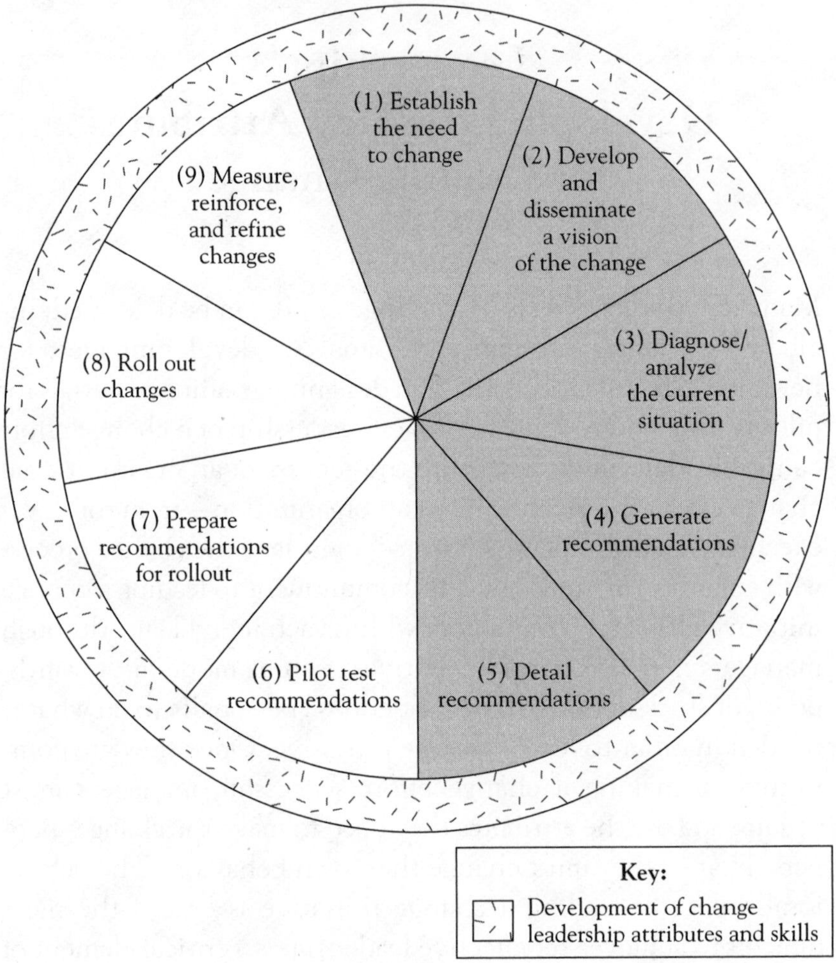

Key:
Development of change
leadership attributes and skills

Relationship Power Versus Position Power

Relationship power, not position power, creates the appropriate environment for change. For years the approach to managing employees could be summed up in a phrase that resembles the title of an old television show: "Manager knows best." Managers told their employees to get a job done and the employees usually did it with no questions asked. Yesterday's managers thus held *position power* over their employees. Management's position power was reinforced through multilayered organizational structures, strict rules and policies, management texts of the day, and general management practice from organization to organization.

Today the situation is different. The last several years have seen a shift in the attitudes of the workforce. People have been changing as rapidly as their environment has. Computers, VCRs, and telecommunications for the masses have given people more access to information, alternative views of the world, and new ways of thinking. The new attitude of today's workforce combined with the flattening of organizations, the teaching of new management models and techniques in universities, and the implementation of alternative management practices means that employees today no longer blindly accept management edicts as they did before. As a result, today's managers must rely much more on *relationship power* than on the position power they once held.

Management based on relationship power requires employee involvement and motivation rather than blind acceptance. Managers who use relationship power build a more committed workforce, elicit stronger loyalty from their people (a quality that is diminishing rapidly in many organizations), and create a more motivated and high-performing team that strives to reach its goals and achieve results. In order to develop relationship power, managers need to embody the key attributes of effective change leaders.

Key Attributes for Leading Change

The behavior of leaders in an organization—that is, what they say and do—throughout all of the nine stages of change has a tremendous impact on whether employees place a high value on making changes work. In other words, the behavior of managers at all levels of an organization can make or break a change initiative. If they fail to do the kinds of things that support a change initiative (for example, make presentations, attend training sessions, hold interactive meetings, provide and listen to feedback, and reward and recognize employees), they send strong negative messages to their organizations, messages such as "Change is only good for other people," or "The leadership of the organization is not committed to the success of the change," and "The changes are not important enough to merit an investment of management time."

Fortunately, managers can also send positive messages about change. Figure 4.2 illustrates six leadership attributes that managers in any organization at any level can embody to promote the process of change. These attributes should be learned, practiced, and applied to help ensure the success of a change effort.

Much has been written on the leadership attributes of effective managers in organizations. (For more information on this, see the recommended readings section at the back of this book.) The attributes described in Figure 4.2 are consistent with this material. These attributes have also been chosen based on my own experiences with effective change leaders in both public and private

Figure 4.2. Key Attributes for Leading Change.

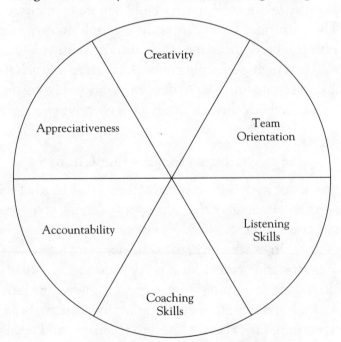

organizations. Effective leaders all possess the six attributes listed and have the skills to apply them effectively to create significant and lasting change in their organizations. When applied to a change process, the attributes identified in the figure will enable managers to instill the belief in the workforce that change is important, that it will be successful, that it will benefit the whole organization (including the employees themselves), and that it will last.

Creativity, the first key attribute of change leaders, includes openness to the creativity of others. Certain actions demonstrate a change leader's creativity, such as developing innovative training processes and offering new incentives that demonstrate the change is different and important. Far more critical to the success of a change effort, however, is a leader's openness to considering and trying new ideas that others come up with during the change process. For example, one team at a large grocery store chain came up with a new restocking method. Several key suppliers would automatically replenish the store shelves with their merchandise when stock fell below a certain level. The suppliers would then bill the chain for the amount of merchandise restocked. The approach would reduce labor costs for the grocery chain significantly and increase the in-stock items in the stores. But when team members brought their ideas to senior management, they were bombarded with unfavorable comments. "It sounds too risky." "We won't know if the suppliers are charging us for stock they really didn't put in the stores." And so on. Even though the team proposed a pilot test of the plan, management held firm and did not let the suggestion go forward. By not even trying out the recommendation, management succeeded only in demoralizing the team. This fact became evident later as the team devoted little effort toward any other task it was asked to perform from that meeting forward.

Yet management could have made other comments instead. "Tell us more." "How can we make it work?" "Let's try it." Had they done so, managers would have sent messages both to the team and to the organization that the company was ready to change, was open to new ideas, and was willing to try new ideas. Openness to the creativity of others provides strong motivation for employees to make a change initiative work.

Team orientation demonstrates a manager's reliance on the help of others to make change happen. The process of organizational change itself dictates that managers cannot make change happen alone. They must enlist others, most often by creating teams. Although the way a leader interacts with teams may vary, all leaders who use teams during a change process must allow the teams to work on tasks without fear of retribution. Change leaders often demonstrate the importance they place on teamwork by attending team meetings, lending a hand to help the team, and regularly letting team members know that the work they are doing is important. An example of this comes from a senior executive at a major oil company. The company established ten teams to redesign various aspects of the business, including information systems, finance, legal, and purchasing. Once a work area was set up, the executive relocated himself to the area in which the teams were working for almost a year, using only a small table with a computer on it for a work space. In addition, when the teams held working meetings, the executive often participated much as an equal member of the team.

Listening is the attribute that communicates to others that their opinions are valued. Often during a change effort, the communication plan concentrates on a one-way flow of information from leadership down to the employees. To be optimally effective during change and beyond, however, communication must be two-way. People need to know that what they say is heard and valued. Accepting input from employees doesn't mean decision making by the masses, however. It means only that people can voice their opinions. Managers need to listen to concerns, suggestions, comments. Although the comments aren't always positive, leaders of a change effort often find that people in the organization aren't as negative as they had feared. Opening channels of two-way communication—such as a special phone number, weekly questions for the president, e-mail, and focus group discussions—provides constructive input into making a change effort operate more smoothly as it progresses.

Coaching may be the most powerful attribute for effecting change. Coaching for performance based on the goals and measures that have been established for the change effort is essential to successful change at all levels of an organization. Without coaching, achievement of the change goals will occur by chance rather than by design. Coaching helps influence the "people variable" in the change process, the variable that is the most unpredictable and, in the end, the one that will have the most impact on success or failure of the effort.

Accountability in the context of change means taking personal ownership for the success of the effort. Managers often take one of two basic approaches to change efforts. When confronted with change, managers can stand back and observe the changes taking place. This approach places change in the context of something done by others. By standing back and observing and, often, criticizing the changes, managers become role models for this kind of behavior. They help create an organization of onlookers rather than participants. When change fails to take hold, the managers who behaved in this manner become the I-told-you-so group in the organization, feeling smug because their opinions about the change efforts proved true. Yet what they have done is help reinforce an organizational culture of stagnation, a culture in which people wait for others to make change happen.

The other approach managers can take is to participate in and support the change process—take ownership of it. Managers who own the changes, participate, and support change with positive input, provide ideas to improve upon it, and offer innovative solutions to the obstacles that inevitably occur during a change process help create and reinforce a culture of organizational learning and growth.

Appreciation allows change leaders to recognize and reward employee efforts to make the change successful. Expressions of appreciation often cost nothing and take little time. Simply offering thanks for a job well done can mean the difference between ongoing success of organizational change and a lack of support for future efforts.

A successful change effort doesn't happen by chance. Both leaders and employees must make an effort to make it happen. If effort goes unrecognized during a change process, the next time effort is needed, it may not be there. Effective change leaders do not wait until the changes have occurred to express their appreciation. They do so frequently along the way. Employees want to know their efforts are being noticed and that they are valued for the work they are doing. Appreciation lets employees know that management values them.

Behavioral Change for Leaders

In order to become effective change leaders, managers must take the steps necessary to acquire and reinforce the attributes needed. Many people believe that the attributes described so far help managers become more successful at leading change. But can these attributes be learned? The answer is yes, but not without practice and reinforcement. Figure 4.3 presents a model for behavioral change that enables managers to develop the attributes of change leaders.

The first step in the behavioral change process is *raising awareness*, that is, the recognition on the part of a manager that he or she can improve a particular behavior or acquire a needed skill. (Appendix A, Strategic Toolkit, question 33.) For example, coaching is described earlier in this chapter as a critical attribute that a change leader should develop. Fortunately, coaching abilities can be learned, practiced, and improved upon over time.

There are many ways in which a manager can take the first step toward awareness. It may come when employees ask for coaching, when a manager takes note of the outstanding results achieved by another manager who effectively coaches employees, when a manager takes a training course that highlights the skills and organizational impact of coaching, or when an executive who serves as a

Figure 4.3. A Behavioral Change Model.

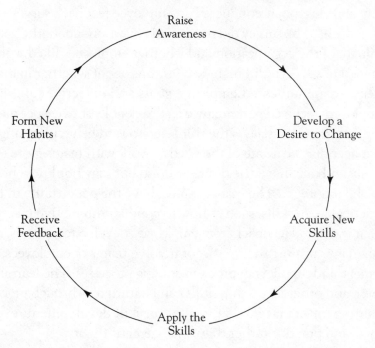

role model takes the time to coach the managers reporting to him or her.

Awareness that leadership attributes such as coaching or listening are important is only the first step in changing behavior. Managers must next *develop the desire to change.* Several factors can instill this desire, including feedback from employees or colleagues indicating that there is a need to change, self-reflection about the impact of one's current behavior on the people with whom one works, and incentives that link goals, measurement, feedback, and rewards and recognition to positive change leadership skills. A good example of this comes from a large telecommunications firm that linked the goals, measurement, feedback, and monetary rewards of management not only to their financial results but also to their ability to lead and develop employees. The company evenly split the rewards for all management between these two factors. It is no surprise that the financial results were the easier of the two factors to track. But the company found a way to assess leadership abilities too: it conducted an employee feedback survey every six months. The survey did not include questions about the general climate of the organization and whether employees liked working there. However, it did include questions about whether managers clearly communicated employee goals and objectives and if the employees received performance feedback at least twice per month.

Acquiring new skills is the third step toward behavior change. A manager may be aware of the need to work with teams more effectively and may have the desire to do so but may not know how to go about doing it. The manager must have the opportunity to learn practical team skills, such as how to conduct interactive meetings, elicit input and feedback from employees, develop team goals, measure teams against their goals, or involve teams of employees, customers, and suppliers in problem-solving processes. The learning of these and other leadership skills can be initiated through practical training for managers that focuses on skill development, experience, and practice rather than management theory.

Managers have to *apply the new skills* once they have learned or improved them. Learning new skills only begins behavioral change. Applying them daily on the job reinforces what has been learned. Regular application helps managers test and improve their skills, see the results achieved, and adjust their behavior as needed. (Appendix A, Strategic Toolkit, question 34.) Moreover, managers like employees need the reinforcement of *feedback* as they practice their skills. (Appendix A, Strategic Toolkit, question 35.) Regular feedback, either from others or oneself, should relate directly to the skills a manager is trying to apply and develop. (Appendix A, Strategic Toolkit, question 36.)

A good example of self-feedback is that of an executive in a large manufacturing company who wanted to learn to express more appreciation to managers and employees. In order to do this, he carried five "appreciation chips" (which resembled plastic poker chips) in his pocket each day. The executive set a personal goal to move all five chips from his right pocket to his left pocket by the end of every day. The rule was that he would move a chip only after expressing some form of verbal appreciation to a manager or employee.

Feedback can also be obtained from supervisors, peers, and employees via 360° surveys—an approach gaining popularity in many organizations today.

Forming new habits is the last step in the behavior change model. New habits are formed when a manager has practiced and refined a skill to the point where it is used automatically rather than through conscious effort and thought. This kind of automatic application of a skill is similar to the ways in which most people drive their cars or tie their shoes. At first the skills involved in such activities need to be consciously practiced and refined. But with consistent and regular practice, the skills become automatic. For example, a manager who decides to improve his or her coaching skills initially needs to remain aware of giving feedback to employees. To reinforce this behavior, he or she may ask others for feedback about coaching skills at the end of each week for two months, then at the end of every two weeks for another two months. Finally, the manager may no longer need this feedback because he or she will have developed the habit of coaching employees on a regular basis.

Summary

To lead change effectively during all of the stages of a change effort, managers today need to develop relationship power within the organization rather than rely on position power. To begin developing relationship power, managers must identify the attributes of an effective change leader and then learn how to acquire or improve upon those attributes in themselves.

However, the leadership attributes that can be acquired through a process of behavioral change are complex. If too many behavioral changes are attempted at once, a manager may find that his or her efforts to change behavior become overwhelming. The behavioral change effort will ultimately fail. Managers who work on acquiring or improving only one or two skills at a time will keep the task manageable and stay focused on it. Restricting efforts to one or two skills at a time does not mean that the others will be neglected. The skills required for leading a change effort are closely interrelated. Coaching skills, for example, are integrally linked to listening skills, team skills, and working relationship skills. Therefore, while focusing on one or two skills, a manager will, at the same time, be strengthening others.

Part Two of the text presents a detailed description of how middle managers and frontline supervisors can apply the attributes and behaviors described in this chapter to ensure the successful implementation and reinforcement of the change effort.

Part Two

At the Grassroots Level

Implementing and Sustaining Change

Chapter Five

Set Goals

The strategic change process is well under way. The rationale for change has been defined, a clear vision has been established, stakeholders have been identified, a communication strategy is working, training is being prepared, and a follow-up plan has been developed. The pilot test phase is starting and rollout is soon to follow. Yet during this grassroots implementation period something is still missing: this is the phase of a change effort when *grassroots change* needs to occur effectively.

Grassroots change creates change deep within an organization by emphasizing implementation at the local level. The primary goal of the grassroots change phase is to implement and sustain desired changes. Readers should remember that the requirements, level of involvement, and goals of strategic and grassroots change differ from one another. Table 5.1 (another version of Table I.1 in the Introduction) reviews the key differences between strategic and grassroots change.

As the table illustrates, the differences between strategic and grassroots change lie in the scope of the effort, the people most heavily involved, and the outcome goals for each level of change. In strategic change, leadership comes from senior levels of the organization. It often involves small teams of select individuals who, using broad diagnostics and analytics together with benchmarking and best-practice comparisons, begin to chart the course, to make recommendations, and to establish momentum for change. Grassroots change involves many more people. The leadership comes from senior executives, middle management, and frontline supervisors.

**Table 5.1. The Differences
Between Strategic and Grassroots Change.**

	Strategic Change	Grassroots Change
Leadership	Top management	Local management
Infrastructure	A select few	Management, employees, "the masses"
Diagnostics	The entire organization	Specific sites
Comparison points	Comparison of external benchmarking and best practices to internal	Implementation of best practices
Tools (process mapping, surveys, activity-based costing, and so on)	Introduction and application of data collection tools and techniques to a select few	Application of implementation tools to "the masses"
Training	Assessment of needs, some design and delivery	Assessment of needs, extensive design and delivery
Outcome goals	Recommendations for change and momentum building	Implementation of changes

During the grassroots change phase, individual and team goals are set, measurements are developed, people are trained and coached in new techniques, procedures, and technologies, reinforcement is established, and changes are implemented.

Grassroots change happens through the management and employees on the front line of the organization, the people who manufacture the products, provide support to the line, or serve customers in the outlets. These are the people who will have to use a new system, follow new procedures, or implement a new manufacturing process. If the new procedures do not take hold, the efforts previously devoted to the strategic change phase will not pay off. One way to help make grassroots change happen is for senior management to issue edicts to the masses: the do-it-and-don't-ask-questions approach. Too frequently this is the approach taken because it is the only one that has already been used and is familiar to the organization. Unfortunately, there are casualties of this approach that often manifest themselves as a drop in morale, problems in labor relations, the exit of key people from the organization, and the inability to attain anticipated results. Luckily, there is another way.

The alternative to the forced-change approach is more motivational, more engaging, and more effective at achieving the results that are expected from the change effort. The approach begins with a focus on the people who must make the changes happen and then make them stick—frontline employees and management. This approach is illustrated in the change implementation model shown in Figure 5.1. Although grassroots change is primarily the responsibility of middle managers and frontline supervisors, using the change implementation model for effective grassroots change is the responsibility of *all* management within an organization, from top to bottom.

In Part Two of the book—Chapters Five through Eight—I address the tools and techniques of the change implementation model that middle managers and frontline supervisors can use to effect change within their spans of control during implementation.

Figure 5.1. The Change Implementation Model.

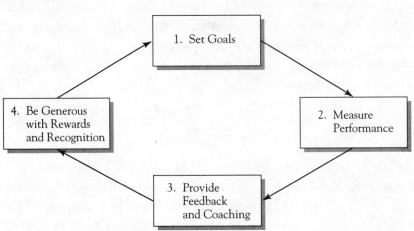

(Appendix B, Implementation Toolkit.) These tools and techniques include goals (Chapter Five), measurement (Chapter Six), coaching and feedback (Chapter Seven), and rewards and recognition (Chapter Eight).

Understanding and Communicating the Changes That Will Take Place

Before beginning the process of applying the change implementation model within their own areas, managers and supervisors must first understand and communicate to their teams the changes that will take place. The first step is to determine what information will be needed to understand the changes more clearly. Managers and supervisors must also gain a good understanding of their personal roles and their teams' roles in implementing the changes. (Appendix B, Implementation Toolkit, question 1.) Once they have a clear understanding, they must identify how they will communicate the changes to their teams—by holding team meetings or passing out written information, for example. (Appendix B, Implementation Toolkit, question 2.) In addition to communicating, managers and supervisors should develop a mechanism for soliciting feedback from their teams about the changes taking place, including a method to feed the information they receive from employees back up to senior management. (Appendix B, Implementation Toolkit, question 3.) As part of the feedback mechanism, managers and supervisors should create a plan of ways in which they can act on the information their teams provide. (Appendix B, Implementation Toolkit, question 4.)

Setting Goals.

A lack of goals creates problems. Without clear goals, people will usually do one of three things: wander aimlessly through the workday looking for "jobs" to keep them busy; run like crazy from one task to another without really accomplishing anything; or wait to be given a task and, when done with it, wait for another to be handed to them. When managers have people working for them who do any of the three, these people need direction—goals.

There are numerous reasons why setting goals should be a priority when undertaking the grassroots aspects of a change effort. First, goals help motivate people. It is widely known that motivated people get more work done and enjoy working. Moreover, they feel a sense of accomplishment and have more initiative to solve the problems and overcome the obstacles that come along with change. Motivated employees are concerned with quality of workmanship. They are dependable and responsible. Motivated people are generally happier and more fun to be around and to work with. Finally, motivated people require less management time. How many managers do we all know who need more time, especially during periods of change? Motivated employees can be relied upon to make changes happen more effectively. Managers don't have to spend huge amounts of time looking over the shoulders of motivated employees to ensure that everything is being done and done right.

The process of goal setting is also imperative to achieving desired changes within an organization. However, the use of individual and team goals in a change process for frontline employees and management is frequently overlooked. Senior management often establishes goals for the change project overall and often for teams working on the initiative. But management frequently does not require goals to be set that support the larger change effort by the rest of the organization. Establishing clear goals allows people to plan a course of action and helps them avoid confusion. This is especially important during a change process when everyone in the organization should be moving in the same direction. Specific change goals supporting the vision of change that are established at the beginning of a change effort should cascade down through an organization. (See Figure 5.2.)

Establishing specific goals for individuals and for teams of managers, supervisors, and employees helps create motivation to implement desired changes within the front line of an organization and

Figure 5.2. The Change Vision.

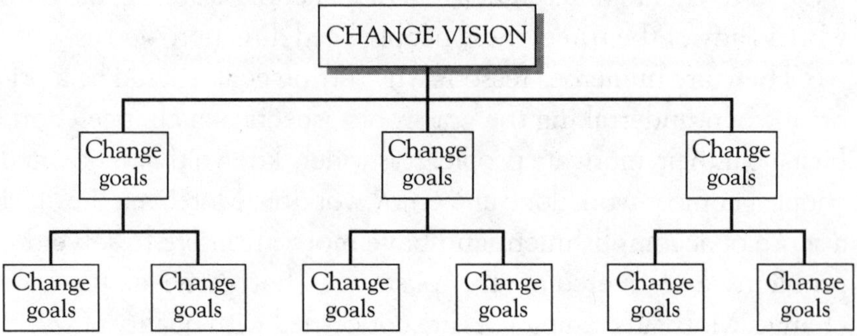

thus is integral to the process of grassroots change. (Appendix B, Implementation Toolkit, question 5.) Figure 5.3 identifies the stages of the change process model—the pilot test and roll-out stages—during which change goals need to be established for front-line management and employees.

An example of effective goal setting for the front line of an organization comes from a large retailer who aligned the customer service goals of all employees, supervisors, and management with the broad goals of the company's change initiative, which was to improve the customer service ratings of the organization by ten points on a service measurement scale. Every employee, supervisor, and manager in the company went through specially designed customer service training. During the training, service behaviors were taught and specific goals for customer service were communicated and set. The result was an increase in customer service ratings of more than fifteen points on the company's scale. And more important, there was an increase in revenues for the company of more than 5 percent over the previous year despite it being a very difficult period for the industry.

Guidelines for Effective Goal Setting

Goal setting is the clear and succinct explanation of what people are expected to achieve in a given time frame. The following are eight essential elements of effective goal setting.

Figure 5.3. The Change Management Process Model.

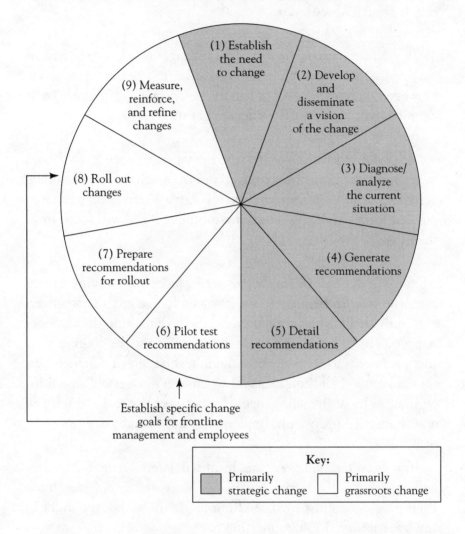

1. *Keep it short and simple (KISS)*. Managers will do themselves and their teams a huge favor by keeping each change goal short, simple, and understandable.

2. *Create goals that are in line with goals developed at the strategic change level*. The change goals that are set during the grassroots change process need to support the vision and direction of the changes at the strategic level in order to achieve the broader goals

of the organization for the change effort. (Appendix B, Implementation Toolkit, question 6.)

3. *Make goals achievable.* The manager and his or her team may not achieve every change goal that it sets out to achieve. However, each team needs to feel that every goal is attainable or its members will not make the effort to get there.

4. *Make goals challenging.* The manager's change goals should be a stretch for both the manager and the team. Goals should be achievable but they shouldn't be too easy. When people have to put out some effort, they become motivated and will learn from their experience.

5. *Involve the team in the goal-setting process.* Involving a team from the start in helping to set its own change goals (both team and individual) will help establish buy in to making the changes happen. The process begins with communicating the change goals the team needs to achieve but shouldn't stop there. Team members should be asked for their ideas. The manager must establish buy in; without it, he or she will struggle to motivate the team to achieve any change. (Appendix B, Implementation Toolkit, question 7.)

6. *Set a time limit.* A time limit will keep a team focused by adding a key motivational dimension. Moreover, people can track their progress against the time limit along the way. (Appendix B, Implementation Toolkit, question 8.)

7. *Establish right away "What's in it for me?"* People work for rewards. To gain commitment from a team, in addition to involving them in setting their own change goals, a manager must establish up front what is in it for them when they reach their goals. They will want to understand both the team and individual rewards. (The discussion of rewards and recognition in Chapter Eight addresses this key factor in more detail.) Managers must

think about rewards and recognition at the start of the process, not at the end.

8. *Clearly communicate the change goals*. The team's change goals should be published for all to see. They shouldn't be a secret. They may be posted on walls or published in a newsletter (with the stale old memo format avoided if possible). Visible change goals do two things. First, they keep people aware of their goals. Second, they communicate to everyone that the change goals are important and that it is important to achieve them. (Appendix B, Implementation Toolkit, question 9.)

I once read a goal statement that helped to point out the essential elements of effective goal setting. It went something like this: "The goal of the billing department is to increase our productivity and reduce our error rates through improved teamwork, better systems, more appropriate allocation of labor hours, lower absenteeism, higher motivation and enhanced commitment to the job." This statement was a classic example of a goal statement that no one could get their arms around. The entire team was confused from the start. The statement was really a goal within a goal within a goal. The author was well meaning, but because of the statement's complexity he was doomed to failure before he even began. He would have done himself and his team a huge favor by breaking the statement down into several clear and concise stand-alone goals. For example, "Over the next six months, the billing department will . . .

1. Improve productivity by 10 percent

2. Reduce error rates by 20 percent

3. Measurably improve teamwork

4. Improve our systems capabilities

5. Allocate labor hours that fall in line with our work needs

6. Reduce absenteeism by 5 percent

7. Measurably improve motivation

8. Measurably enhance our team members' commitment to the job

Short, clear, concise goals such as these provide people with bite-size chunks that they feel are *achievable*.

In addition to being short and simple, each of these goals includes an essential characteristic: a time limit. The eight billing department goals share a six-month time limit. A time limit provides two important things. It tells people the date at which the goal must be achieved and it allows them to track their progress continually. People can monitor their progress as often as they wish—daily, weekly, monthly, and so on. Doing this helps them determine if they are on track in meeting the deadline. A time limit is a key motivator for people. An excellent example of this is the two-minute drill at the end of a football game. Countless times we see teams get their adrenaline pumping, pull together, and march eighty yards to the winning score simply because they know their time was running out. Why does this happen? It happens because they know their goal (to score more points than the other team) and they know how long they have to achieve it (sixty minutes total with only two left to go).

The eight billing department goals provide one example of simple goal setting. Obviously the team needs to clarify each goal further, for example, more clearly define what they mean by motivation in goal number seven. The discussion should also include how to measure each goal. (Measurement techniques will be addressed in detail in the next chapter.) Any conversation between the department manager and the team should take place before the billing department's goals are finalized. During that discussion the manager begins to get buy in and commitment from the team members.

The following section presents three more simple examples of goal setting: one from Rags Retail Unlimited, a second from the Stand-Alone Construction Company, and a third from the Multi-manufacturing Corporation.

Rags Retail Unlimited

Rags Retail Unlimited will measurably improve our customer service standards over the next six months by

- Reducing customer waiting time in all departments by 20 percent
- Reducing customer phone service waiting time by 20 percent
- Reducing returns/exchange service processing time by 20 percent
- Reducing check out processing time by 10 percent
- Using the customer's name during all credit transactions
- Saying hello and thank you to 100 percent of our customers
- Reducing our negative comments on customer surveys by 50 percent
- Increasing our positive comments on customer surveys by 20 percent
- Smiling while on the sales floor

The Stand-Alone Construction Company

During the central building project our team will

- Complete the project ahead of schedule, in under eighteen months
- Beat our project budget by 10 percent
- Keep our team safety rating at 100 percent for the entire project
- Maintain measurable standards of quality workmanship
- Keep our team absentee rate below 5 percent of the total labor days

Multimanufacturing Corporation

The Multimanufacturing Corporation will measurably improve our assembly process over the next six months by

- Reducing our rework rate by 25 percent

- Reducing our start-to-finish processing time by 10 percent

- Reducing our backlog of work in process by 50 percent

- Allocating our labor resources to better match work flow needs

- Cross-training all our employees in at least one other key process skill

- Reducing our absentee rate by 10 percent

Summary

Effective goal setting begins the process depicted in the change implementation model. Change goals should be established during the pilot testing and roll-out stages of the model. Specific change goals should support the broader goals of the change effort. Clear change goals help establish the motivation for frontline management and employees to make the changes happen in their areas and set the stage for the accomplishment of the final stages of change implementation: measuring performance, providing feedback and coaching, and offering rewards and recognition.

Chapter Six

Measure Performance

After clear change goals have been established, the next step in implementing change is to measure performance against those goals. There are two important reasons for measuring performance during a process of change. First, it is necessary to be able to determine when goals have been achieved. Once there is a clear understanding of what the change goals are (both broadly and specifically), measurement allows determination of whether they have been accomplished. Has the organization reduced absenteeism, increased customer service, come in under budget, or improved teamwork? Without reliable measurement, these questions cannot be answered credibly. There would only be guesses. Measurement removes the guesswork.

Second, measurement provides a way to track progress. When what needs to be measured and the way to measure it are known, managers can see for themselves whether the organization is on track in achieving its change goals. Accomplishing change goals shouldn't come as a surprise to anyone. Periodic measurement allows awareness of progress toward change goals. People can observe the achievement of milestones along the way. Obtaining intermediate landmarks helps them stay motivated and keeps them committed to achieving the change goals that have been established. Measuring progress against change goals should occur during stage six (pilot testing) and stage nine (measure, reinforce, and refine changes) of the change process model. (See Figure 6.1.)

Figure 6.1. The Change Management Process Model.

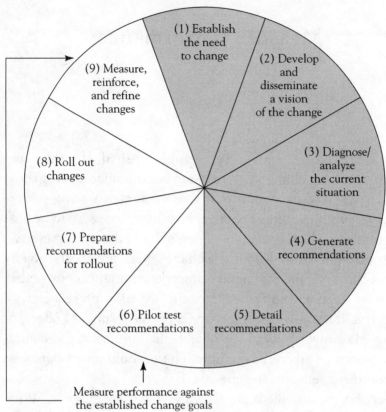

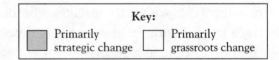
Measure performance against
the established change goals

Key:

▨ Primarily
strategic change

☐ Primarily
grassroots change

Guidelines for Effective Measurement

There are several guidelines for accomplishing effective measurement:

1. Set specific, numeric expectations.

2. Keep it simple (KISS).

3. Be creative.

4. Involve people in designing their own measurements.

5. Determine the frequency of the measurement.

6. Determine who will be responsible for keeping score.

As the guidelines indicate, the first rule of measurement is to set specific, numeric expectations. (Appendix B, Implementation Toolkit, question 10.) People become more motivated when they can see results. Many people think it is impossible to provide clear numeric measurements for activities. When they make this assumption they are defeated before they start. In fact, any activity can be measured in time, units, money, or customer satisfaction. It is true that measuring customer satisfaction isn't as clear-cut a process as counting the strokes in a golf game. However, readers should remember something important: *if there is no effort made to measure it, it is not worth wasting the time to try to manage it* because there will always be questions about whether the situation is improving from one day to the next.

Creativity is needed in order to come up with measurements for intangible change goals such as improved customer satisfaction, better teamwork, enhanced communication, and higher morale. Creativity is the key that unlocks new methods of measuring old issues and helps avoid the "same old measurement for the same old issues." A good example of this is in the area of customer service. A "typical" approach to measuring customer service improvement is counting customer complaints. The traditional way of "improving service" is reducing the number of complaints. However, this method of measurement can easily backfire.

For example, one company that attempted to reduce the number of complaints found that its people were induced into suppressing and ignoring customer gripes rather than dealing with them. The company had caused this by implementing a reward system based on measuring complaints. As a result, the employees didn't act to correct customer problems but hid them instead. The company actually lost sales because employees were not taking action to correct the problems.

Another company took a more creative approach to measuring service. A branch manager for a regional retail chain was assigned to a store notorious for poor performance. One thing she noticed when she took over the store was the poor attitude of the staff toward customer service. She decided to begin measuring the service her team gave to the customer. She knew that many people thought the best way to measure service would be by sales; more sales meant better service. However, she realized that there are many reasons why people buy and service is just one of them. Yet she still wanted somehow to begin to manage service. The branch manager asked her people—those closest to the customers—to devise a way to measure service. Her team came up with five attributes that could be measured on a rating scale of 1 to 10: (1) smiling, (2) looking neat and clean, (3) making at least one nonbusiness comment during each transaction, (4) saying hello and thank you at the beginning and end of every customer interaction, and (5) using the customer's name. The salespeople then began to rate one another. Everyone achieving 80 percent or more in a given week received a reward. The branch manager also gave out rewards for the top scoring service achiever each month. Within a few weeks, she noticed a friendlier atmosphere in her store. Many customers actually commented on the excellent service they were receiving. After just three months, her store's financial performance improved significantly.

This is an example of an excellent way to devise creative measurements to measure the immeasurable: *involve the team*. By involving the team in defining its own measurement criteria, managers will be amazed at the credible and creative approaches that will be developed. (Appendix B, Implementation Toolkit, question 11.) If the team is asked to, it will generate many ideas—some good and some not so good. Furthermore, as in the process of goal setting, when people are encouraged to define their own measurement, commitment and buy in to tracking their own performances are gained.

Keeping it simple is the second important guideline in establishing measurements. Complex measurement systems only confuse and alienate people. For example, one measurement system for tracking the individual performance of sales staff put in place by a clothing chain included sales performance versus last year, sales per hour, total sales to date for the week and the month, sales against target, increase of sales trend from month to month, units per sale, and average sale value. All of this was felt by senior management to be useful information. Managers of the outlets were asked to track and discuss this information on a regular basis with each of their salespeople. Some information was to be discussed daily, some weekly, and some monthly. The system failed for two reasons.

First, frontline management spent huge amounts of time compiling and calculating the information. Second, the sales staff was overwhelmed and confused by the barrage of data. In a very short time, the company found that no one was using the system. The idea was scrapped completely. The company would have been much better off if it had kept it simple, prioritizing the most important measures and then asking managers and staff to track just one or two of the key aspects that related to individual selling performance, such as daily and weekly total sales. (Appendix B, Implementation Toolkit, question 12.) The point is to keep measurement simple so that people use it and pay attention to it.

Finally, two aspects of measurement that should never be overlooked are frequency and responsibility. Once measurements are established, frequency of measurement must be set and an individual chosen to be responsible for keeping score. (Appendix B, Implementation Toolkit, questions 13 and 14.) The manager should consider rotating this responsibility. Doing so will help people stay aware of the score as they progress and will also alleviate the tendency for one person to become burned out by being the only one who tracks the team's progress. For individual goals and measurement, individual responsibility should be assigned to each person to keep his or her own score.

Measurement is nothing more than keeping score. By regularly keeping score, progress can be assessed against a given standard. Keeping score provides a point of comparison. For example, in a golf game, golfers know after every hole how they are doing against three standards: (1) the other players in their group, (2) their own score the last time out on the course, and (3) the par set for each hole.

What Does Measurement Look Like?

There are no limits to the way measurement can look. Here are a few examples to help spark ideas.

Self-Rating

Asking teams and individuals to rate themselves on whatever factors are determined to be important is a good way to approach measuring immeasurables like customer service, teamwork, and communication. Many managers find that the ratings their team members give themselves are often more critical than the ratings the managers themselves would have given them. Self-rating offers several important positive aspects. First, it establishes buy in to the measurement technique. Second, it motivates people as it becomes important to them. Third, although self-rating may not be minutely accurate, an awareness is created around the facets that are being rated. Awareness is the first step toward change and improvement.

Measurement of Discrete Behaviors

Measuring discrete behaviors will also work with intangibles like communication, teamwork, and service. Measuring behaviors can be as simple as determining whether a team of bank tellers regularly say thank you or tracking the amount of time a manager mingles with the loading dock team each day. Improved communication, teamwork, or service has to "look like" something. These kinds of behaviors are what communication, teamwork, and service look like.

Visual Measurements

People are visual. They like to see what is happening around them. Visual measurements are a good way to keep people motivated and interested in their performance. A creative example of this comes from a company that wanted to develop a novel approach to decrease spending. At the beginning of each month the company distributed what it called "budget bucks" to each of its department heads. The amount each department received was equal to its budget for that month. Employees were asked to staple the "money" to expense vouchers and also to use it to "purchase" supplies from the company stockroom. Department heads submitted the budget bucks with requests for checks to pay invoices. By raising awareness the company hoped to reduce expenses as a percent of sales by 3 percent. However, as people became more aware of cash flow through this visual system, expenses actually fell by over 5 percent.

Wall charts are another example of visual measurements. Posted prominently and kept up to date, wall charts that track key performance measures are an effective way of displaying a score board of team progress. Used appropriately, wall charts stimulate interest and enthusiasm to improve and achieve goals. (Appendix B, Implementation Toolkit, question 15.) Figure 6.2 shows a wall chart used to track errors in an order entry department.

Summary

Measuring performance against the change goals that have been established is the second step in the process described by the change implementation model. Measurement should be conducted

Figure 6.2. Order Entry Department Daily Error Rates: Wall Chart.

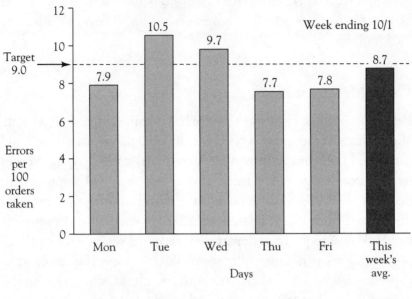

Last week's average = 10.2
This week's target = 9.0

during stages six (pilot testing) and nine (measurement, reinforcement, and refinement of changes) of the change process model. Several guidelines should be followed when establishing and conducting measurement during a change effort: specific, numeric, expectations should be set; measurements should be kept simple; responsibility for keeping score should be assigned; measurements should be made visible; frequency of measurement should be set; and creative measures should be developed for intangibles such as teamwork or communication.

Goal setting and measurement go hand in hand. Together, they lead to the next step in the change implementation model: providing feedback and coaching.

Chapter Seven

Provide Feedback and Coaching

After establishing clear change goals and measurement techniques, the next step in the change implementation model is feedback and coaching. People need feedback to learn, to grow, and to improve. Without feedback, learning and change occur haphazardly at best and stagnate at worst. When an individual, team, or organization stops learning, performance stops improving. Feedback and coaching enable people to adjust regularly their efforts toward achieving the established change goals. Ongoing adjustment by managers and employees alike is extremely important when changes are being implemented because few changes will be achieved successfully by most people on the first try: achieving change is a learning process. Figure 7.1 shows that feedback and coaching should occur regularly during stage six (pilot testing) and stage nine (measurement, reinforcement, and refinement) of the change process model.

If coaching is so integral to the success of implementing changes, why don't more managers and supervisors at all levels apply the techniques of coaching as often as they should? Many times it is their assumptions that limit their effectiveness as coaches. In most instances, these are unconscious assumptions; people are unaware they even exist. For example, people possess limiting assumptions about offering positive feedback to others, including the following:

- If I give positive feedback it might embarrass people.
- People know themselves when they are doing well.
- If I give positive feedback they might start to slack off and take advantage of me.

Figure 7.1. The Change Management Process Model.

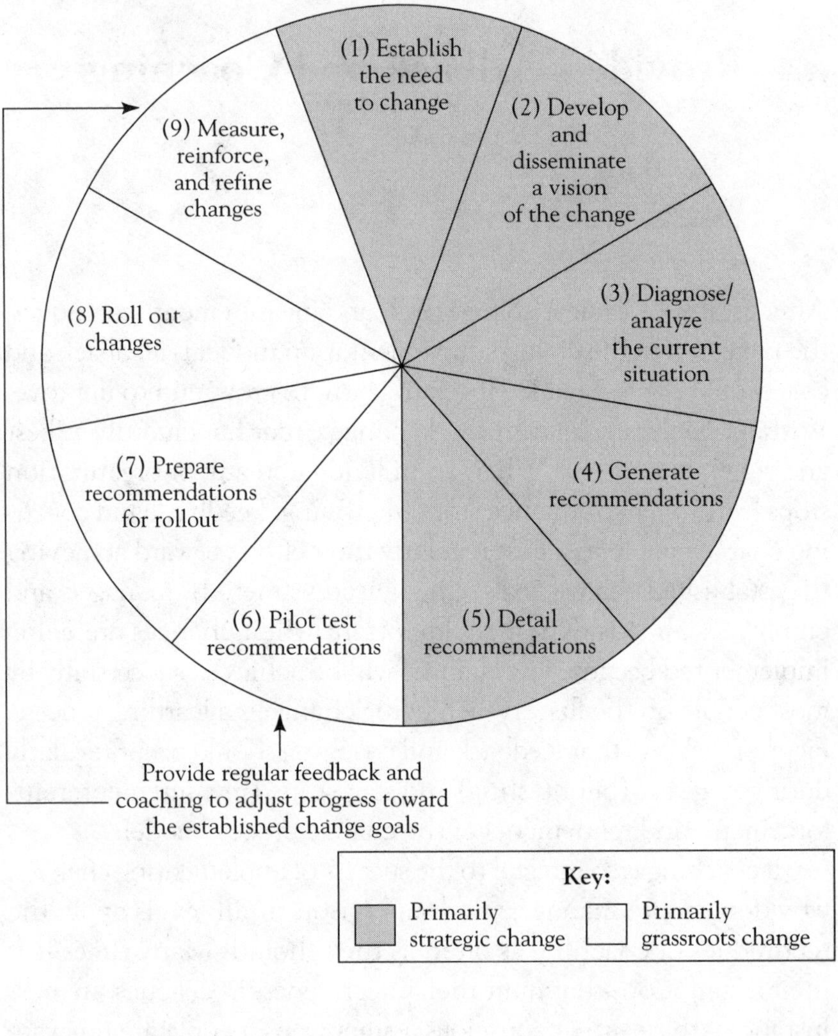

They might ask for a raise.

- They might ask for a raise.
- I might sound insincere.

People also possess limiting beliefs about constructive feedback, such as the following:

- People may be upset if I give them constructive feedback.
- They may get defensive.

- Constructive feedback may demoralize them.
- They should know by themselves what needs to improve.
- They may think I'm being too critical.

Managers are paid to develop people and, in times of change, help them achieve the goals. If they don't do this, managers are not really doing their jobs. Feedback and coaching are needed at all levels and in all organizational types in order to develop people and help them accomplish the changes that need to be made. Feedback creates awareness.

Posting a chart of daily or weekly sales performance is a form of giving feedback. (Using this type of feedback is described in more detail in Chapter Six.) Watching a videotape of a presentation that one has conducted is feedback. Pointing out to a cashier that he or she always says hello and smiles at the beginning of each customer transaction is also feedback.

In coaching, feedback is used to help people become aware in order to capitalize on their strengths and improve upon their weaknesses. Thus, coaching is both positive and constructive. For example, suggesting that the same cashier continue to greet each customer with a hello and a smile helps him to capitalize on his strengths (smiling and saying hello to each customer). This kind of suggestion is an example of positive feedback and coaching. During the same discussion, suggesting that offering a thank you at the end of each transaction would make him even better at his job is an example of constructive feedback. Using feedback as a base, coaching enables managers and supervisors to help people improve their performance.

What Do Feedback and Coaching Look Like?

Feedback and coaching "look" very different from individual to individual. Just as each coach of a sports team develops his or her own style, every manager should develop his or her own style of coaching. Fortunately, all individuals have a resource to draw upon to help them start becoming better coaches: the experience they themselves have had in being coached by other people. Thinking back to the coaches one has had in the past can help an individual learn to become a better coach. Past coaches were not necessarily sports coaches, but they were people who enabled an individual to learn and grow through their comments, actions, and guidance. These coaches may include parents, teachers, friends, and so on. By identifying the traits that past coaches possessed and the helpful things they did, an individual can begin to incorporate those actions. Attributes usually identified in good coaches are trustworthiness, persistence, empathy, belief in themselves and in others, openness, consistency, and a tendency to offer both positive and constructive comments. Finally and most important, everyone needs to apply and improve that coaching style continually.

Guidelines for Effective Coaching

There are no set rules for coaching. However, effective coaching has several typical attributes. A set of guidelines follow. (Readers should remember that, like the rest of the chapters in Part Two of the book, these guidelines are intended for managers and frontline supervisors to use to effect change within their spans of control during the implementation process. Thus they focus on communication within their teams.)

● *Before coaching anyone, establish up front that coaching will take place with everyone.* Taking this approach leaves no surprises that coaching will take place. Each person knows that he or she is included. (Appendix B, Implementation Toolkit, question 16.)

● *Make coaching timely.* It is best not to wait too long to coach people. The impact of the specific examples offered will be lost with time. The nearer to the occurrence of the activity, the better. (Appendix B, Implementation Toolkit, question 17.)

- *Do your best to make people feel comfortable enough to coach you.* It is a good idea to ask for coaching from the person one reports to, from peers, and from employees. The more feedback we receive, the more we learn. (Appendix B, Implementation Toolkit, question 18.)

- *Don't criticize.* Coaching is not criticism. Before making comments, a manager needs to know how he or she feels. When upset with something or someone, it is better not to try to coach someone because it will only be a negative experience for both parties. It is better to wait to cool down and gather one's thoughts. Coaching looks ahead to improve on people's current abilities, enabling them to learn from mistakes and successes. Coaching is motivating. Criticism is demoralizing.

- *Keep it simple and informal.* Coaching should not be complicated. The format should be informal. There is no need for pens and paper. The two people should sit facing each other; without the typical office barriers or "power desks" between them, the coaching discussion is often much more open and productive. In addition, both individuals should try to stay focused while delivering or receiving coaching.

- *Choose an appropriate time and location without interruptions.* The right moment and a good location will encourage openness.

- *Be specific.* The discussion should be limited to work-related behavior, the things people do and say that affects their performance and the achievement of change goals. People can change their behavior. Specific suggestions for improvement help people understand more clearly what it is that they need to adjust to keep improving.

- *Keep coaching balanced.* Both positive, "You are effective because . . ." and constructive, "You could be even more effective if . . ." comments should be made.

- *Be empathetic.* A good coach puts herself in the other person's shoes. She remembers how it was when she was trying to learn the job.

- *Encourage team members to coach one another about the changes they are making.* If team members coach one another, it takes some of the burden off the team leader. Moreover, managers can develop future leaders by teaming up more senior members of your team with more junior members to establish a coaching relationship. However, it is important not to use this approach in order to get around having to be a coach oneself. (Appendix B, Implementation Toolkit, question 19.)

A Coaching Tip

The following paragraphs offer managers a useful approach to coaching that they can apply right away.

- Write down the names of five co-workers that you yourself would like to receive feedback and coaching from for your personal improvement. They may be people you report to, peers, or subordinates.

- Ask one of the people on the list to sit down with you for ten minutes to exchange feedback and coaching. Explain the purpose of the conversation. Let the individual know that you would like to exchange ideas about how both of you can improve your work performances—both in areas where you each do well and in areas where you can improve. Allow the individual at least a few minutes to gather thoughts along these lines. Make sure you let him or her know that you wish to have an informal discussion for improvement purposes, not for criticism.

- The meeting should feel informal. Choose a place and time

where you won't be interrupted. Don't sit behind your desk; remove the barrier of the "power desk." Sit facing each other.

•   You and the other individual then take turns providing feedback and coaching. Decide who will coach for the first five minutes and who will coach for the second five minutes.

•   Several opening statements help lead into positive and constructive comments. To begin a positive comment, the lead may be: "You are effective because. . . ." Then go on to describe to the person you are coaching a few of the specific things that he does that you believe makes him effective in his job. This is the positive side of coaching. These comments should be followed with the statement, "You would be even more effective if . . ." after which a few of the specific things that the person you are coaching can do to improve are mentioned. This is the constructive side of coaching.

It should be noted that the lead phrase maintains a positive tone by using the words "even more effective," indicating that the person is already effective and that what follows are just suggestions in ways you feel they can improve.

•   Throughout the conversation, check that you are both maintaining a positive and supportive tone aimed at helping each other learn and improve. The listener, or the person who is being coached, should listen and receive the comments in a positive way. The listener should remember that coaching is meant for learning and improvement, not criticism. There is no need to get embarrassed by positive comments or to try to justify or explain behaviors when receiving constructive comments.

•   At the end of the conversation, thank the person for his suggestions and agree to continue to coach each other on a regular basis. Then repeat the same process with all the other people on your list.

Summary

Providing feedback and coaching as people attempt to implement change helps tremendously in achieving the change goals that have been established. Most people will not be successful in using a new system, following a new procedure, or changing their service behaviors on the first, second, or even third tries. In the same way that it helps athletes, feedback and coaching help employees improve with each subsequent attempt. Regular feedback and coaching should be provided during stages six (pilot testing) and nine (measurement, reinforcement, and refinement) of the change process model. Several guidelines should be followed when providing feedback and coaching: establishing up front that coaching will occur with everyone, keeping feedback timely, being open to feedback and coaching oneself, not criticizing, keeping coaching simple and informal, and being specific with suggestions for improvement. When managers and supervisors approach the process of feedback and coaching in this way on a regular and consistent basis, it helps establish a culture of support and learning in an organization and markedly improves performance while achieving the changes to be made.

Chapter Eight

Be Generous with Rewards and Recognition

The last step in the change implementation model is to provide rewards and recognition. Rewards and recognition are needed primarily to provide reinforcement when people are successful at implementing changes. Rewards and recognition are often what people focus on as they strive to achieve their goals. When goals center on implementing changes, rewards and recognition help reinforce the achievement of those goals and, ultimately, help sustain the implementation of the changes to be made.

Another important reason to reward and recognize people during a process of change is to help motivate them to implement changes in the future. If they are not rewarded and recognized for the work they put in to accomplish the goals of a change effort, they will be much less willing to put in the same amount of effort the next time a change process is undertaken.

In addition, rewards and recognition tell people that their work is appreciated. We all remember those times when we put in the effort to complete a really tough job and all we really wanted to hear was the boss say the words "thank you"—but never did. Most managers will explain this behavior by saying something like, "I don't need to say thank you, my team knows I appreciate the effort they put in." But when their team members are asked about it, the answers given are often very different.

The Difference Between Rewards and Recognition

There is a basic difference between rewards and recognition. *Rewards* are what people receive for completing a task or reaching a goal. Rewards are tangible symbols of appreciation for a job well done. They can take the form of cash, perks, stock, trips, and so on. *Recognition* is how people know the effort they put into their work has been noticed. Recognition can occur at a personal level between a manager and a team. The manager may gather the team together at the end of an effort and announce team and individual achievements. Rewards may also be presented at this time.

Recognition can also be broader, occurring at the division or company level. Team and individual accomplishments may be announced at division or company meetings. Accomplishments can be published in the company newspaper. In addition, senior executives may be asked to visit a team to recognize its achievement. Rewards and recognition should be linked to achievements as key milestones are met and change goals are achieved throughout implementation—during stages six (pilot testing) and nine (measurement, reinforcement, and refinement) of the change process model. (See Figure 8.1.)

Guidelines for Effective Rewards and Recognition

The following paragraphs offer some useful guidelines for providing rewards and recognition.

• *Directly link rewards and recognition to performance and the achievement of change goals*. People should not have to wonder what the payoff will be when they perform and achieve change goals. Directly linking rewards and recognition to making changes happen helps establish clarity of purpose. (Appendix B, Implementation Toolkit, question 20.)

• *Involve people in designing rewards*. A good source for developing rewards and recognition is the people in the organization themselves. Asking people what they would like to see as payoff for performance can generate a lot of creative ideas. They should be realistic when suggesting rewards, but they shouldn't be limited too

Figure 8.1. The Change Management Process Model.

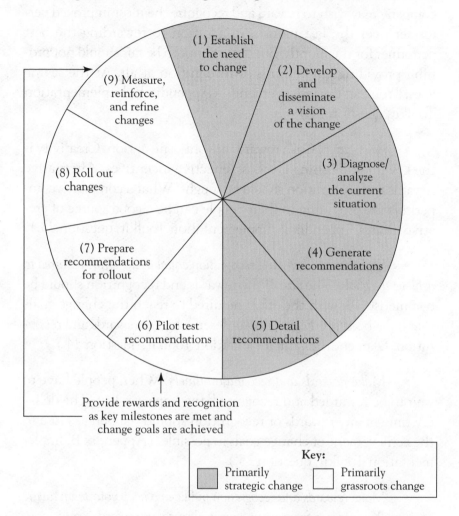

much. They are only making suggestions. Indeed, managers may be surprised at how inexpensive many ideas that seem costly at first glance turn out to be. (Appendix B, Implementation Toolkit, question 21.)

• *Try to make rewards and recognition fair for everyone.* The opportunity to receive rewards and recognition should be as equal as possible. Whatever the criteria established, the equality of the process for receiving rewards should be gauged. For example, a company may wish to reward and recognize the most improved performer over the last month, in addition to rewarding the best performer for the month. But the attempt to be fair should not prohibit providing any rewards or recognition at all. As the saying goes, "You can't please everyone." (Appendix B, Implementation Toolkit, question 22.)

• *Be creative*. Cash rewards are only one option. Creativity is the key to establishing low cost, effective incentives. Alternative rewards and recognition should be sought. What a company's competitors are providing to their people can be a good source of creative ideas. (Appendix B, Implementation Toolkit, question 23.)

• *Make the rewards and recognition equal to the effort required to achieve the goals*. The size of the rewards and recognition should be commensurate with the effort required to reach the change goals that have been set. Bigger efforts deserve bigger rewards and recognition. (Appendix B, Implementation Toolkit, question 24.)

• *Make rewards and recognition timely*. When people have to wait to be rewarded and recognized, the impact is lost. The delivery time of any rewards or recognition should happen as close to the achievement of change goals as possible. (Appendix B, Implementation Toolkit, question 25.)

• *Make rewards and recognition public and keep your team aware of them*. Keeping information secret about the rewards and recognition that people will receive only defeats its purpose. Letting people know the payoff and keeping them aware of it throughout the change effort will help to keep them focused and motivated to achieve the change goals. (Appendix B, Implementation Toolkit, question 26.)

• *Communicate success once change goals are achieved*. Communicating successes to management and the rest of the organization once change goals are achieved instills a sense of accomplishment in the people who have been successful. This kind of communication also sends messages to others in the organization that there is a payoff to carrying out change effectively. (Appendix B, Implementation Toolkit, question 27.)

• *Offer a few well-placed words of praise and appreciation: they will go a long way.* Often people want and need to hear a few words of appreciation on the way to achieving a goal, especially when the road to accomplishing a change goal is a long one. Even though their main goal may not be achieved for months or longer, saying something to people such as "I really appreciate the effort you have all put in this week" on a Friday before they go home lets them know their hard work has been noticed. Appreciation like this helps a team stay motivated throughout all efforts. Managers need to remember to take the time to stop, get people listening, and be sincere when providing appreciation.

• *Remember the magic words.* Whatever rewards and recognition are developed, two words often go the furthest in communicating appreciation to others: "Thank you."

What Do Rewards and Recognition Look Like?

Although it may be true that the reason people accept a job offer is the pay, once on the job, money is usually not the only reason they perform. Rewards and recognition can take many forms besides cash. The business world offers abundant examples of creative, unique, and effective rewards and recognition. Examples include additional training, a share in the business, trips, pictures and articles in the company newspaper, plaques, paid vacation time, lunches and dinners, complimentary letters and visits from executives, participation on improvement teams, trophies, office equipment and furnishings, schedule changes, new work assignments, and so on.

When cash is in short supply, the key is to be creative. One excellent technique to design creative rewards is to ask people within the organization for help. They may have suggestions for the types of rewards that they would like to receive. When team members help develop their own rewards they are more likely to become motivated to receive them.

Summary

The observant reader will have noticed the abundant use of gaming and sporting analogies throughout this and the previous three chapters, all of which dealt with implementation during grassroots change. Why was this done? Simply because people enjoy games and sports. They enjoy them because games motivate through excitement and fun. When people are playing their favorite game they feel an adrenaline boost and their efforts increase. There are a few key reasons for this.

First, when they play a game, people know the goals. They know right from the start of a game what they are setting out to achieve and how long they have to get there. Second, they know how to measure their progress. In any game people know how to keep score: through goals, touchdowns, runs, baskets, points, and so on. Third, they regularly receive feedback and coaching. They are also constantly reminded of what the score is, that is, how they are doing every step of the way. They either see the feedback on a score board, hear it from spectators or a coach, or keep themselves aware as they progress. And in addition to receiving constant feedback about the score, they often get coaching on how to improve skills, techniques, and strategies during the game, that is, coaching that is aimed at helping to improve both performance and score. This coaching often comes from other players, from team captains or coaches, and from instructors who are giving lessons. Finally, people get rewarded and recognized for their efforts. They hear the praise of the coach, the cheers of the spectators. And they feel the satisfaction within themselves of a game well played.

The analogies with games and sports are intended to imply that human performance can similarly be managed during a process of organizational change. This can be done by making work and the process of change more motivating and, potentially, *even fun*. It is a generally held belief that a company cannot motivate anyone, that all it can do is establish an atmosphere that will foster the individual's own internal motivation and allow it to flourish. Effectively applying the four steps of the change implementation model enables organizations to establish that atmosphere while undergoing change.

Conclusion

The Tough Questions of Change Management

This book has attempted to provide readers with a pragmatic and comprehensive approach to addressing the human aspects of change. However, some questions may still remain. Questions often asked by management include the following: Why should our organization change at all? When do we stop a change effort if it isn't working? How do we deal with the natural resistance people have to change? These are all good questions and I will address each one here.

First, why should an organization change at all? The answer is, There is no choice. The competition is getting stronger every day. In all industries, a standard of continuous learning and improvement is being pursued and becoming the norm. In addition, major change is being achieved by organizations across the globe. Change is resulting in dramatic improvements in service, huge reductions in operating expenses, and enormous leaps in revenue and profits.

Second, when should a change effort be stopped if it isn't working? For the reasons listed in the previous paragraph, organizations can't stop change. However, readers should understand that it is part of the normal process that a change effort will experience difficulty. No matter how hard one tries, one cannot please everyone—members of senior management, middle management, frontline supervisors, employees, unions, shareholders, and so on. Accepting that there will be difficulty (especially regarding the soft side of change) is paramount to undertaking and continuing a change effort. Otherwise, we either give up when difficulty arises or are paralyzed before we start. *The Human Side of Change* is intended to help minimize the human problems encountered along the rocky road of change.

How do we deal with the natural resistance people have to change? *The Human Side of Change* aims to provide management at all levels with tools, techniques, and lessons learned to help overcome the normal resistance people have to change. The book intends to illustrate to an audience of senior executives, midlevel managers, and frontline supervisors how they can navigate through the pitfalls surrounding the human elements of change in order to create a successful transformation, a lasting transformation that achieves desired outcomes and allows people at all levels to see change as a positive thing to do both for themselves and for the organization as a whole.

Each chapter in the book presented actions that executives, managers, and supervisors can take to manage the human elements during a change effort, including using teams to develop and test changes, forming and executing a complete change communications strategy, linking organizational culture to the implementation of changes, developing the core attributes management needs to lead change initiatives effectively, and using goal setting, measurement, feedback and coaching, and rewards and recognition to implement and advance changes within an organization.

The steps and actions described in each chapter are most often not linear in practice. For example, a communications strategy cuts across all stages of a change process, as does the development of management attributes to lead change. Likewise, pilot testing of some changes may take place as other change recommendations are still being developed. Because organizational change is iterative, managing change (especially the soft side of it) is more akin to conducting an orchestra than to accomplishing a series of steps like those in a paint-by-numbers kit. It would be naive to consider almost any change effort simplistic. Repeated experience shows that a simplistic, one-dimensional approach that focuses only on the technical aspects of an organization creates significant problems that then manifest themselves when labor relations issues arise, benefits of the change are limited or nonexistent, change goals are not achieved or are short lived, and key people leave the organization.

To ensure success management must consider and plan for all aspects of a change process from the outset, not when the initiative is already under way. Unfortunately, although most executives and managers are adept at the operational, financial, and systems aspects of organizational change they are not proficient at managing the people aspects. This situation exists for several reasons: the emphasis on quantitative analysis found in most business school curriculums, the focus by management on the technical side of organizations (as historically demonstrated and reinforced through management promotion and reward criteria), and the complexity and ambiguity of managing people (an uncomfortable topic for most executives and managers to address).

Moreover, unlike equations, managing the soft side of change often does not yield immediate, observable, results. Some people learn faster than others. People have varying likes and dislikes, and hold diverse beliefs about the way an organization should operate and the way work should get done. All of these human differences must be taken into account and managed during a change initiative. By applying the actions described in the previous chapters throughout a process of change, organizations can successfully combine the technical and people aspects of change to create a more effective and lasting transformation.

The Change Manager's Toolkit

Appendix A

Strategic Toolkit

This workbook is for use by senior executives and senior managers. Its purpose is to provide a guide for managing the strategic aspects of organizational change, as described throughout Part One of this book (Chapters One through Four).

The questions on the pages that follow offer prompts for the key actions needed to manage effectively the strategic aspects of a change initiative, including the following:

- Defining the need to change
- Developing a vision of the result of change
- Leveraging teams to design, test, and implement changes
- Developing and executing a communications strategy
- Addressing the cultural aspects of the organization that will help implement and sustain change
- Developing the essential attributes and skills needed to lead the change effort

As an additional aid to the users of this workbook, each question is referenced to the corresponding chapter within the text to which it applies.

Defining the Need to Change

1.   (Introduction) What are the driving needs to undertake the change effort? For the company? For employees? Others?

(Answers may include desire for excellence, competitive pressures, the results of benchmarking, organizational survival, customer satisfaction, and so on.)

2. (Introduction) How long has this need existed? (The answer to this question will communicate the urgency to change.)

3. (Introduction) How will you communicate the need to change? Who will you communicate it to? (The answer will provide information for the communication strategy.)

Developing a Vision

4. (Introduction) What is the vision of how the organization will look like after the changes have taken place? (For example, it will become a global organization with 50 percent of the business outside of the United States.)

5. (Introduction) What is the time frame for achieving the vision?

6. (Introduction) How will you involve people in establishing the vision for change?

7. (Introduction) How will you communicate the vision of the change? Who will you communicate it to? (The answer will provide information for the communication strategy.)

Establishing a Steering Committee

8. (Chapter One) Who should lead the steering committee?

9. (Chapter One) Who should be included on the steering committee?

10.   (Chapter One) What is the role and responsibility of the steering committee? (The answer may be direction, issue resolution, allocation of resources, and so on.)

11.   (Chapter One) How often will the steering committee meet? (For example, once a week, twice a week, once a month, twice a month, and so on.)

Establishing Improvement Teams

12.   (Chapter One) What teams are needed? (For example, teams to redesign processes, teams to design a new organization structure, and so on.)

13.   (Chapter One) Who should the leader of each team be? What is the time commitment to the team? (For example, 20 percent of the individual's time, 50 percent, 100 percent.)

14.   (Chapter One) Who will facilitate each team's working process to keep it focused and meeting deadlines? (For example, a member of each team, external consultants, internal facilitators, and so on.)

15.   (Chapter One) Who should be included on each team? What is their time commitment to each team? (For example, 20 percent of their time, 50 percent, 100 percent.)

16.   (Chapter One) How will the current workload of the team members be covered during their commitment to the change initiative?

Developing and Executing a Communications Strategy

17.   (Chapter Two) Who are the stakeholders in the change? (For example, management, employees, customers, share holders, the community, and so on.)

18. (Chapter Two) What objectives do you want to accomplish by communicating with each of the stakeholders? (For example, buy in from management, understanding of the changes and new skills from employees, awareness of the changes by share holders, and so on.)

19. (Chapter Two) What are the key messages you want to send to each stakeholder to accomplish the above objectives? (For example, new roles, new methods, new skills, the impact on service, financial impact, and so on.)

20. (Chapter Two) What communication vehicles do you want to use for each stakeholder? (For example, face-to-face meetings, training sessions, written information, news releases, and so on.)

21. (Chapter Two) At what frequency should the messages be delivered? (For example, once during the beginning of the initiative, weekly, monthly, and so on.)

22. (Chapter Two) Who will be accountable for developing and delivering the messages? (For example, executives for delivery, communications department to develop, training department to develop and deliver, and so on.)

23. (Chapter Two) How will you ensure that two-way communication happens (that is, feedback upward as well as messages downward)?

24. (Chapter Two) How will you ensure that communication and feedback continue once the changes occur?

25. (Chapter Two) How long after going live will communication and upward feedback about the changes continue?

26.   (Chapter Two) What mechanisms will be used to determine and take appropriate actions to respond to feedback?

Linking Organizational Culture to the Recommended Changes

27.   (Chapter Three) Which cultural components identified from the cultural screen will be applied to help implement and sustain the desired changes? (For example, setting new goals and measurement, developing new rewards and recognition, establishing new training, supplementing communications, redefining rules and policies, and so on.)

28.   (Chapter Three) What specific implementation actions have you developed for each cultural component (identified in number 27) that applies to the change?

29.   (Chapter Three) What is your implementation action plan that focuses on successfully leveraging each cultural component (identified in number 27) to implement and sustain the desired changes?

30.   (Chapter Three) Are you adhering to your implementation action plan (developed in number 29), including using all the resources, people, and timing indicated in the plan?

31.   (Chapter Three) What quantitative and qualitative measures will you use to provide a complete picture of the effectiveness of the changes being implemented?

32.   (Chapter Three) How will the culture of the organization be continuously managed once the changes have taken place? Who will be accountable for managing it?

Developing the Skills to Lead the Change Process

33.   (Chapter Four) Which leadership attributes will you work on during the change process to improve your skill in leading change? (For example, listening, coaching, appreciation, and so on.)

34.   (Chapter Four) How often will you work on the attributes you identified in number 33? (Daily, weekly, and so on.)

35.   (Chapter Four) From whom will you solicit feedback about your own progress against your behavioral change objectives? (Your supervisor, peers, employees, others.)

36.   (Chapter Four) How and how often will you solicit feedback from the people you listed in number 35? (In written surveys, one on one meetings, team meetings, and so on.)

Appendix B

Implementation Toolkit

This workbook is for use by middle managers and frontline supervisors. Its purpose is to provide a guide for managing the grassroots aspects of organizational change, as described in Part Two of the book (Chapters Five through Eight).

The questions on the pages that follow offer prompts for the key actions needed to manage effectively the grassroots aspects of a change initiative, including the following:

- Understanding and communicating the changes to employees
- Setting goals
- Measuring performance
- Providing feedback and coaching
- Establishing rewards and recognition

As an additional aid to the users of this workbook, each question is referenced to the corresponding chapter within the text to which it applies.

Understanding and Communicating the Changes

1.   (Chapter Five) What information do you need to understand more clearly the changes to take place and your and your team's role in implementing the changes? (Answers may include technical information, time frame, organizational goals of the change, how your team fits into the changes, and so on.)

2.   (Chapter Five) How will you communicate your understanding of the changes to your team? (For example, team meetings, written information, ask for an executive to meet with your team, and so on.)

3.   (Chapter Five) How will you solicit feedback from your team about the changes and how will you feed that information up to your manager, both before and after the changes take place?

4.   (Chapter Five) How will you act upon the information that your team provides to you about the changes they are implementing?

Setting Goals

5.   (Chapter Five) What are the top five change goals you will use to begin the process of goal setting with your team?

6.   (Chapter Five) How will you incorporate the vision of change that has been set for the organization into the change goals of your team?

7.   (Chapter Five) How will you set both individual and team goals with your employees regarding the implementation of the changes to take place? (For example, hold a meeting with each individual or the team as a whole, use the draft set of goals from question number 5 to begin a discussion with the team, ask each team member to submit draft goals to you for you to edit, and so on.)

   a. Plan to develop individual team member goals.

   b. Plan to develop team goals.

8.   (Chapter Five) What time frame will you set to accomplish the goals? Is your team's time frame in line with the change time frame of the organization?

9. (Chapter Five) How will you keep you and your team aware of the goals that are set? (For example, publish a copy for each team member, post the goals on walls, review the team's progress against the goals in weekly or monthly team meetings, and so on.)

Measuring Performance

10. (Chapter Six) What specific, numeric, measurements will your team use to determine progress toward achieving the change goals that have been set?

11. (Chapter Six) Which measures (identified in question 10) will you prioritize to keep your measures down to a manageable number?

12. (Chapter Six) How will you involve your team in determining their own measures?

13. (Chapter Six) How often will the measurements be updated? (For example, daily, weekly, and so on.)

14. (Chapter Six) Who will be responsible for keeping the measurements up to date for your team? How often will you rotate this responsibility?

15. (Chapter Six) How will you keep your team and others aware of progress? (For example, reporting back progress during weekly meetings, hanging up wall charts, and so on.)

Providing Feedback and Coaching

16. (Chapter Seven) How will you introduce to your team that coaching and feedback will take place for everyone?

17.   (Chapter Seven) How often will you coach your team members?

18.   (Chapter Seven) How will you encourage your team to coach you, too?

19.   (Chapter Seven) How will you encourage your team members to coach one another to achieve the changes to take place? (For example, team up senior members of your team with junior members.)

Offering Rewards and Recognition

20.   (Chapter Eight) What rewards and recognition will you use to reinforce the achievement of your team's goals and implementation of the changes?

21.   (Chapter Eight) How will you involve your team in determining their own rewards?

22.   (Chapter Eight) How will you attempt to make the rewards that are chosen fair for everyone? (For example, offering a "most improved" award.)

23.   (Chapter Eight) What creative rewards or special recognition will you use to let your team members know they are doing a good job at implementing the changes? (For example, lunches, executive visits, frequent "thank yous.")

24.   (Chapter Eight) How will you ensure that the rewards and recognition are equal to the effort required to achieve the goals? (Bigger efforts deserve bigger rewards.)

25.   (Chapter Eight) How will you ensure that the rewards and recognition are given in a timely way, as soon as possible after change goals have been achieved?

26.   (Chapter Eight) How will you keep yourself and your team aware of the rewards during the process of change?

27.   (Chapter Eight) How will you communicate to management your team's success in achieving their goals and implementing changes? How will you communicate it to the rest of the organization? (For example, through the company newspaper, broadcast messages on e-mail, and so on.)

Glossary of Terms

Activity-based costing: A method of identifying the resources (for example, people, materials, and cost of human labor) allocated to a particular business process.

Benchmarking: The quantitative measurement and comparison (for example, costs, cycle time, or labor) of an organization's business processes against competitors and other organizations with similar processes.

Best practices: The qualitative comparison (for example, methods, procedures, technology, organizational structure, and rules and policies employed) of an organization's business processes against competitors and other organizations with similar processes.

Business process reengineering (BPR): Fundamental rethinking of business processes that often creates entirely new processes, combines several processes, functions, or jobs into one process, and results in step change for organizations.

Business processes: The transformation of inputs (for example, information or raw materials) through machines, people, energy, and information systems that result in desired outputs.

Change management: The techniques used to create and sustain changes within an organization.

Communications vehicles: The various media used to convey messages out to and receive messages back from identified stakeholders (for example, written and electronic messages, video, face-to-face discussions and presentations, conference phone calls, and so on).

Continuous improvement: Incremental change that is structured and ongoing, typically resulting in modest innovations (for example, limited cost savings or service improvements) to confined areas of an organization.

Cost-benefit analysis: The determination of the costs (for example, capital, people, time, and equipment) of making changes to a business process versus the potential benefits (for example, expense reduction, revenue growth, customer service improvements, and cycle time reductions) that are identified from making the changes.

Cycle time: The duration of time from the beginning of a business process (when inputs are received) to the end (when outputs are available).

Facilitation: Assistance provided to improvement teams to increase their ability and effectiveness in conducting meetings, using analytical techniques and tools, and applying decision-making procedures.

Improvement team: A group of people (for example, management, employees, and customers) who pool their resources, skills, knowledge, and abilities in order to achieve a common goal.

Stakeholders: People who have an interest in or will be affected by a change effort.

Step change: Significant change that results in dramatic improvements in service, reductions in operating expenses, or leaps in revenue and profits.

Appendix D

Recommended Readings

General Material on Organizational Change

Eales-White, R. "The Dimensions and Dilemma of Change." *Industrial and Commercial Training*, 1993, 25(9), 28–36.

Gardner, D. M. "Breakpoints: How Managers Exploit Radical Business Change." *Journal of Marketing*, Oct. 1993, pp. 152–153.

Glover, H. D. "Organizational Change and Development: The Consequences of Misuse." *Leadership and Organization Development Journal*, 1992, 13(1), 9–16.

Imparato, N., and Harari, O. "When New Worlds Stir." *Management Review*, Oct. 1994, pp. 22–28.

Kirkpatrick, D. K. *How to Manage Change Effectively.* San Francisco: Jossey-Bass, 1985.

Kyle, N. "Staying with the Flow of Change." *Journal for Quality and Participation*, July/Aug. 1993, pp. 34–42.

LeClerc, R. J., and Daniels, A. "Managing Change." *Canadian Business Review*, Winter 1993, pp. 17–20.

Lippitt, G. L., Langseth, P., and Mossop, J. *Implementing Organizational Change.* San Francisco: Jossey-Bass, 1985.

Mink, O. G., Esterhuysen, P. W., Mink, B. P., and Owen, K. Q. *Change at Work.* San Francisco: Jossey-Bass, 1993.

Mohrman, A. M., and others. *Large-Scale Organizational Change.* San Francisco: Jossey-Bass, 1989.

Smith, B. "Business Process Reengineering: More than a Buzzword." *HR Focus*, Jan. 1994, pp. 17–18.

Swist, J., and Ayers, A. "Managing Hidden Aspects of Change." *Transportation and Distribution*, Nov. 1994, p. 84.

Troy, K. "Change Management: An Overview of Current Initiatives. A Research Report." The Conference Board, 1994, pp. 1–46.

Wade, J., Rosenthal, J., and Hall, G. "How to Make Reengineering Really Work." *Harvard Business Review*, Nov./Dec. 1993, pp. 119–131.

Teams

Bottom, W. P., and Baloff, N. "A Diagnostic Model for Team Building with an Illustrative Application." *Human Resource Development Quarterly*, Winter 1994, pp. 317–336.

Davies, R. "Team Building: An Exercise in Leadership." *International Journal of Career Management*, 1995, p. v.

Dyer, W. G. *Team Building Issues and Alternatives*. Reading, Mass.: Addison-Wesley, 1987.

Fox, W. M. *Effective Group Problem Solving*. San Francisco: Jossey-Bass, 1987.

Hatch, E. K. "Cross Cultural Team Building and Training." *Journal for Quality & Participation*, Mar. 1995, pp. 44–49.

Parker, G. M. *Cross-Functional Teams*. San Francisco: Jossey-Bass, 1994.

Varney, G. H. *Building Productive Teams*. San Francisco: Jossey-Bass, 1989.

Woodcock, M. *Team Development Manual*. (2nd ed.) London: Gower, 1989.

Communications

Beck, C. E. "Perspectives on the Self in Communication." *Technical Communication*, Nov. 1994, pp. 753–759.

Bryan, J. "Glue for the Reengineered Corporation." *Communication World*, Aug. 1994, pp. 20–23.

Ettorre, B. "An Ounce of Prevention." *Management Review*, Apr. 1995, p. 6.

Glanz, B. A. *The Creative Communicator*. Chicago: Kaset International, 1993.

Koonce, R. "The 'People Side' of Organizational Change." *Credit Magazine*, Nov./Dec. 1991, pp. 22–24.

Luft, J., and Ingham, H. *Group Processes: An Introduction to Group Dynamics*. Mountain View, Calif.: Mayfield, 1984.

Zener, M. F., and Smeltzer, L. R. "Organizationwide Change: Planning for an Effective Announcement." *Journal of General Management*, Spring 1992, pp. 31–43.

Organizational Culture

Atkinson, P. E. "Culture Change: Familiarity and Back to Basics." *Management Services*, Feb. 1994, pp. 18–20.

Clement, R. W. "Culture, Leadership, and Power: The Keys to Organizational Change." *Business Horizons*, Jan./Feb. 1994, pp. 33–45.

Kilmann, R. H., Saxton, M. J., and Serpa, R. *Gaining Control of the Corporate Culture*. San Francisco: Jossey-Bass, 1985.

Hope, V., and Hendry, J. "Cultural Change and Competitive Performance." *European Management Journal*, Dec. 1994, pp. 401–406.

Schein, E. H. *Organizational Culture and Leadership*. San Francisco: Jossey-Bass, 1992.

Simpson, P., and Beeby, M. "Facilitating Public Sector Organizational Culture Change Through the Processes of Transformational Leadership: A Study Integrating Strategic Options Development and Analysis with the Cultural Values Survey." *Management, Education, and Development*, Winter 1993, pp. 316–329.

Leading Change

Conger, J. A., Kanungo, R. N., and Associates. *Charismatic Leadership*. San Francisco: Jossey-Bass, 1988.

De Bono, E. *Lateral Thinking: Creativity Step by Step*. New York: HarperCollins, 1970.

De Bono, E. *Serious Creativity: Using the Power of Lateral Thinking to Create New Ideas*. New York: HarperCollins, 1992.

Duck, J. D. "Managing Change: The Art of Balancing." *Harvard Business Review*, Nov./Dec. 1993, pp. 109–118.

Flower, J. "Human Change by Design." *Healthcare Forum*, July/Aug. 1992, pp. 84–89.

Gabarro, J. J., and Athos, A. G. *Interpersonal Behavior, Communication, and Understanding*. Englewood Cliffs, N.J.: Prentice Hall, 1978.

Koestenbaum, P. *Leadership*. San Francisco: Jossey-Bass, 1991.

Kotter, J. P. "Leading Change: Why Transformation Efforts Fail." *Harvard Business Review*, Mar./Apr. 1995, pp. 59–67.

O'Toole, J. *Leading Change*. San Francisco: Jossey-Bass, 1995.

Pickering, J. W., and Matson, R. E. "Why Executive Development Programs (Alone) Don't Work." *Training and Development*, May 1992, pp. 91–95.

Ray, M., and Myers, R. *Creativity in Business*. New York: Doubleday, 1986.

Sonneberg, F. K. "The Age of Intangibles." *Management Review*, Jan. 1994, pp. 48–53.

Stace, D., and Dunphy, D. "The Strategic Management of Corporate Change." *Human Relations*, Aug. 1993, pp. 905–920.

Stewart, T. A. "Managing Change: How to Lead a Corporate Revolution." *Fortune*, Nov. 28, 1994, pp. 48–61.

Tichy, N. M. "Revolutionize Your Company." *Fortune*, Dec. 13, 1993, pp. 114–118.

Von Oech, R. *A Kick in the Seat of the Pants*. New York: HarperCollins, 1986.

Von Oech, R. *A Whack on the Side of the Head*. New York: Warner Books, 1990.

Welch, J. F., Weiss, W., Walsh, M., and Bossidy, L. "A Master Class in Radical Change." *Fortune*, Dec. 13, 1993, pp. 82–90.

Goals

Galpin, T. J. "How to Manage Human Performance." *Employment Relations Today*, Summer 1994, pp. 207–225.

Manning, D. J., Jr., and Martin, B. A. "Combined Effects of Normative Information and Task Difficulty on the Goal Commitment–Performance Relationship." *Journal of Management*, Spring 1995, pp. 65–80.

Moravec, M., Juliff, R., and Helser, K. "Partnerships Help a Company Manage Performance." *Personnel Journal*, Jan. 1995, pp. 104–108.

Riggs, J. "Empowering Workers by Setting Goals." *Nation's Business*, Jan. 1995, p. 6.

Measurement

Coonradt, C. A. *The Game of Work*. Shadow Mountain, 1984.

Meyer, C. "How the Right Measures Help Teams Excel." *Harvard Business Review*, May/June 1994, pp. 95–103.

Norton, D. P., and Kaplan, R. S. "The Balanced Scorecard—Measures That Drive Performance." *Harvard Business Review*, Jan./Feb. 1992, pp. 71–79.

Norton, D. P., and Kaplan, R. S. "Putting the Balanced Scorecard to Work." *Harvard Business Review*, Sept./Oct. 1993, pp. 134–147.

Feedback and Coaching

Bartlett, R. C. "The Mentoring Message." *Chief Executive*, Mar. 1995, Issue 101, 48–49.

Geiger-Dumond, A. H., and Boyle, S. K. "Mentoring: A Practitioner's Guide." *Training and Development*, Mar. 1995.

Hoffman, R. "Ten Reasons You Should Be Using 360-Degree Feedback." *HR Magazine*, Apr. 1995, pp. 82–85.

Laborde, G. Z. *Influencing with Integrity*. New York: Syntony, 1987.

Millsap, R. E., and others. "An Examination of the Effects of an Upward Feedback Program over Time." *Personnel Psychology*, Spring 1995, pp. 1–34.

O'Reilly, B. "360-Degree Feedback Can Change Your Life." *Fortune*, Oct. 17, 1994, pp. 93–100.

Rewards

Brooks, S. S. "Noncash Ways to Compensate Employees." *HR Magazine*, Apr. 1994, pp. 38–43.

Hogarty, D. B. "New Ways to Pay." *Management Review*, Jan. 1994, pp. 34–36.

Kanin-Lovers, J. "Should Compensation Lead or Lag Organizational Change?" *Journal of Compensation and Benefits*, Sept./Oct. 1993, pp. 45–48.

Kurland, O. M. "Recent Trends in Compensation Planning." *Risk Management*, Nov. 1992, pp. 76–77.

O'Neill, D. "Blending the Best of Profit Sharing and Gainsharing." *HR Magazine*, Mar. 1994, pp. 66–70.

Wolters, D. S., and others. "Rethinking Rewards." *Harvard Business Review*, Nov./Dec. 1993, pp. 37–49.

Index

A

Ability, and resistance to change, 43–45
Accountability: in communications, 48, 50–51; and leadership, 73; for measurement, 97
Achievability, of goals, 88, 90
Analysis. *See* Diagnosis and analysis stage
Appreciation: and leadership, 73–74, 76–77; in rewards and recognition, 113
Arena, in communications, 35–37
Awareness: from feedback, 103; and leadership, 74–75; and measurement, 99

B

Balance, and coaching, 105
Behaviors: leadership changes in, 74–77; measurement of discrete, 98–99; observing, and culture change, 63
Benchmarking: concept of, 135; and need to change, 5; for recommendation generating, 8
Best practices: concept of, 135; for recommendation generating, 8
Blindspot, in communications, 36–37
Bremen, University of, and resistance hierarchy, 43
Business process reengineering: concept of, 135; and need to change, 5

C

Change: developing desire to, 75–76; difficulties of, 117–118; as iterative, 118–119; levels of, 1–3, 11–12; need to, 4–5, 12, 17–18, 117, 123–124; reinforcing, 63–65; resistance to, 42–45, 118; and team infrastructure, 17–18; time frame for, 4; understanding and communicating, 84, 129–130

Change management: aspects of process for, 1–13; and communications, 34, 46; concept of, 135; culture in, 54–55, 57; details recommended in, 4, 9, 12; diagnosis and analysis in, 4, 7–8, 12; feedback and coaching in, 102; glossary on, 135–136; and goal setting, 87; at grassroots level, 79–115; issues in, 117–119; and leadership, 68; measurement, reinforcement, and refinement in, 4, 10, 12, 94; model of, 3–10, 12; and need to change, 4–5, 12; pilot testing in, 4, 9–10, 12; readings on, 137–141; recommendations generated in, 4, 8–9, 12; rewards and recognition in, 111; rollout recommendations in, 4, 10, 12; rollout stage in, 4, 10, 12; at strategic level, 15–78; summary on, 11–13; toolkit for, 121–141; and vision development and dissemination, 4, 5–7, 12
Coaching: aspects of, 101–108; attributes of, 103–104; exercise in, 106–107; guidelines for, 104–106; and leadership, 73; readings on, 140; reasons for, 101–103; summary on, 108; toolkit for, 131–132
Communications: aspects of, 33–52; framework for, 33–39; fundamentals of, 39–41; for goals, 89; by improvement team, 25; Johari Window for, 34–37; listening in, 72–73; matrix for, 48; open and two-way, 35–37; phases in process of, 45–47; pitfalls in, 41–42; readings on, 138; resistance lowered by, 42–45; for rewards and recognition, 112–113; specific strategy for, 47–51; summary on, 51–52; toolkit for, 125–127; and understanding change, 84, 129–130; vehicles for, 48, 50, 136

Content, for communications, 48, 49–50

Creativity: and leadership, 71–72; in measurement, 95–96, 99; in rewards and recognition, 112, 114

Culture: action plans in, 58, 61; aspects of managing, 53–65; in change management, 54–55, 57; components of, 53–54, 56–58, 59–60, 62; implementing actions in, 58–62, 64–65; measuring impact of changing, 62–63; readings on, 138–139; and reinforcing change, 63–65; as screen, 55–58, 62; summary on, 65; toolkit for, 127

D

Details recommended stage: in change management, 4, 9, 12; cultural screening in, 55–58

Diagnosis and analysis stage: in change management, 4, 7–8, 12; communication in, 38, 40; and improvement team, 25–26

E

Equity, in rewards and recognition, 111–112

Exposure, in communications, 37

F

Facade, in communications, 36–37

Facilitation: concept of, 136; for improvement teams, 23, 25, 26, 30–31

Feedback: assumptions about, 101–103; and coaching, 101–108; in communications, 37, 40–41, 51; on culture change, 63; readings on, 140; toolkit for, 131–132

Filters, in communication, 40

G

Games, analogies with, 114–115

Germany, and resistance hierarchy, 43

Goal setting: aspects of, 81–92; examples of, 91–92; guidelines for, 86–92; need for, 84–85; readings on, 140; summary on, 92; toolkit for, 130–131

Grassroots change: aspects of, 79–115; background on, 81–84; concept of, 2, 3, 11–12; at diagnosis and analysis stage, 8; feedback and coaching in, 101–108; goal setting in, 81–92; goal of, 81; implementation model of, 83; measuring performance for, 93–100; and pilot testing, 9; rewards and recognition in, 109–115; at rollout stage, 10; toolkit for, 129–133

H

Habits, for leadership, 77

I

Implementation, for action plans, 58–62, 64–65. See also Grassroots change

Improvement teams: aspects of, 21–32; concept of, 136; facilitation for, 23, 25, 26, 30–31; members of, 23–24; operations of, 24; principles for, 29–30; priority matrix for, 22; process for, 24–29; proposal from, 27–28; record keeping by, 31–32; results from, 22–23; toolkit for, 125; work of, 21–22

Infrastructure. See Team infrastructure

Ingham, H., 33–34

Integration team, in team infrastructure, 19, 20–21

J

Johari Window, for communications, 33–37

K

Knowledge, and resistance to change, 43–45

L

Leadership: aspects of, 67–78; attributes for, 69–74; behavioral change for, 74–77; commitment to, 67; power in, 68–69; readings on, 139; summary on, 77–78; toolkit for, 128

Listening, and leadership, 72–73

Luft, J., 33–34, 35n

M

Management, and grassroots change, 79–115. See also Change management

Maslow, A., 43

Measurement: aspects of, 93–100; in change management, 4, 10, 12; creativity in, 95–96, 99; of culture change, 62–63; examples of, 98–99; feedback and coaching in, 101; guidelines for, 94–98; by improvement team, 29; numeric, 95; readings on, 140; reasons for, 93–94; rewards and recognition in, 110; summary on, 99–100; toolkit for, 131; visual display of, 99–100

Motivation, and goal setting, 85–86, 88–89

O

Objectives, for communication, 48, 49
Organizations: communication framework for, 33–39; culture of, 53–65; grassroots change in, 79–115; Johari Window for, 37–38; readings on change in, 137; strategic change in, 15–78

P

Performance: measuring, 93–100; rewards and recognition linked to, 110
Pilot testing: in change management, 4, 9–10, 12; communications in, 45; feedback and coaching in, 101; by improvement team, 28–29; measuring in, 93; rewards and recognition in, 110
Power, relationship and position types of, 68–69

Q

Quality circles, and improvement teams, 21

R

Recognition. *See* Rewards and recognition
Recommendation generating stage: in change management, 4, 8–9, 12; for improvement team, 26–28
Refinement: in change management, 4, 10, 12; and communication, 45, 48, 51
Reinforcement: in change management, 4, 10, 12; of culture change, 63–65

Resistance to change: issues of, 118; pyramid of, 43–45
Resources, for culture change, 61
Rewards and recognition: aspects of, 109–115; difference between, 109–110; forms of, 113–114; guidelines for, 110–113; readings on, 140–141; reasons for, 109; summary on, 114–115; toolkit for, 132–133
Rollout recommendation stage, in change management, 4, 10, 12
Rollout stage: in change management, 4, 10, 12; communications in, 40, 42, 45, 51

S

Self-rating, for measurement, 98
Simplicity: for goals, 87; for measurement, 97
Skills, acquiring and applying, 76–77
Stakeholders: in communication, 47–49; concept of, 136
Steering committee: in team infrastructure, 19, 20; toolkit for, 124–125
Strategic change: aspects of, 15–78; communications for, 33–52; concept of, 1, 3, 11–12; and culture, 53–65; leadership for, 67–78; team infrastructure for, 17–32; toolkit for, 123–128

T

Team infrastructure: aspects of, 17–32; breadth of, 19; coaching by, 106; establishing, 17–19; and goal setting, 88; improvement teams in, 21–32; integration teams in, 19, 20–21; leader orientation toward, 72; and measurement, 96; readings on, 138; steering committee in, 19, 20; summary on, 32
Testing. *See* Pilot testing
Timing: for change process, 4; for coaching, 104; in communications, 48, 50; for culture change, 61; and goal setting, 88, 90; of measurement, 97; of rewards and recognition, 112

U

Understanding change, and communicating, 84, 129–130

Unknown, in communications, 36–37

V

Vehicles, communications, 48, 50, 136
Vision: cascading, 6–7; in change management, 4, 5–7, 12; and goal setting, 86; and team infrastructure, 17–18; toolkit for, 124

W

Wall charts, and measuring, 99–100
Willingness, and resistance to change, 43–45